In His Hands

A Spiritual Journey

OLIE K. TEETER, JR

WESTBOW
PRESS®
A DIVISION OF THOMAS NELSON
& ZONDERVAN

WestBow Press books may be ordered through booksellers or by contacting:

WestBow Press
A Division of Thomas Nelson & Zondervan
1663 Liberty Drive
Bloomington, IN 47403
www.westbowpress.com
844-714-3454

ISBN: 978-1-6642-0716-5 (sc)
ISBN: 978-1-6642-0715-8 (e)

Print information available on the last page.

WestBow Press rev. date: 10/29/2020

Contents

PART II
Doctrine, Teachings & Traditions 101

Introduction

Have you ever read a scripture in the Bible and thought, "That doesn't fit our church doctrine," or wondered, " Why does it says something different in another scripture?" Or does it?

Does the Bible contradict it's self? Or could it be we are looking at the scriptures wrong? Are we being Deceived?

Of all the different denominations and church doctrines how do you know which one has the real truth of God's Word?

Have you ever questioned the doctrine of your Church?

Can you answer this question?

"Do we try to make scripture fit our doctrine or does our doctrine fit the scriptures?

I'll give you a minute to think about that one. It's not a trick question!

How do I know which of the spiritual gifts I have and where is my place in the body of Christ?

Is there a way to know the truth of God's Word when there are so many different traditions and teachings within the churches?

Are any of them right, can we really know?

Let's look at some Doctrines, Teachings and Traditions when tested by Scripture?

Are you up for a challenge?

During my life time I have experienced many of these issues and encounters.

Dreams as a child, God speaking to me and sending people to give me direction.

My encounter with the Holy Spirit!

Dreams/Visions, God sending me to South America on an unknown mission.

Through out my story, I have come face to face with these questions and more. Choices I had placed before me.

My story is no different then anyone else, UNTIL! GOD KNOCKED ON MY DOOR!

That's were the adventure begins!

Even when I wasn't walking with God, He was directing my path. The right place, the right people and the right time.

It's amazing how hind-sight is 20/20!

This is who I am and the path I walk!

Always seeking, but far from perfect!

PART I

When God is Leading

Where to Begin?

Some years ago, well, I guess it would be better to say many years ago, a friend told me," you will write!"

At the time I was a very new Christian still running on the adrenaline of events surrounding the Lord speaking to me. I really didn't think I needed to write anything, for the Lord would give me what I needed to say. As it turns out both are right. There is a place and time for everything!

I guess I would have to say I am compelled to write, not because I am any different or special but because of what God has done in my life, not what I have done.

I was pretty much a normal kid growing up with my share of knocks and bruises. Like most young boys I had no need for girls, oh, I had my cousins but they were family and I didn't think of them as girls!

I was often picked on by some of the older boys in Flintstone but that was normal I guess. I really disliked having to watch my younger brother especially when it interfered with something I wanted to do.

I guess my Mom thought I should have had curly hair as I remember her put my hair in curlers and I hid it under my cowboy hat. My! what a boy has to endure to please his Mother! I still have a picture of me with the curls in my cowboy shirt. I still have the cowboy shirt, but not the curls!

Let me introduce myself, my name is Olie Kenneth Teeter, Jr., but for the first seventeen years of my life I was Junior. Olie was my Dad. When I went away to Electronics School I became another person, I became the son of my father, Olie, Jr! I still have my friends from school and family who still call me Junior, so I know from when someone knew me, before or after High School!

I was born January 3, 1947, in Cumberland, Maryland, Mom was Montre Lugene Beck Teeter and my Dad was Olie Kenneth Teeter, Sr., Mom was 16 years old and Dad was 18 when they were married December 1, 1943. Dad had just joined the Army Air Corp and was going through Cadet Training to be a pilot in World War II, not the best of circumstances to start a marriage. It was wartime and Mom would follow Dad to New Mexico during his time there for training.

Sometime during his Cadet training, the Army pulled half of the Cadets and sent them to Gunner Training. There was a needed for Crews for the new B29 bombers. Dad said after walking through a scrapyard of crashed airplanes the biggest part was the tail section, said that is where he wanted to be. So he became a Tail Gunner.

After finishing training and getting their new B29 they flew to Tinian, a small island in the South Pacific off the coast of Japan. This was one of several Air Base's constructed for the bombing campaign of Japan.

Dad never talked much about the war. Only in his last years did he tell stories mostly of how they got home after the war. His photo album tells another story of life on Tinian, as there were still Japanese soldiers hiding on the island.

At the end of the war, Dad didn't want to come home on a ship, but wanted to fly home. He kept bumping himself back by marking off his war medals so he could fly. To do so they had to rebuild a B29 that had been ditched by another crew, even replacing all four engines. He did get his metals many years later before he died.

Only on the morning of his funeral while going through a box of his papers, did I learn that his plane and crew were one of six that flew with the Enola Gay. The day the first Atomic Bomb was dropped.

After the war Mom and Dad lived in Chaneysville, Pa. for a short time until I was born. Then while living in a cabin on Town Creek, I almost died of pneumonia and we moved sometime thereafter. Dad worked various jobs in the area, worked in a junkyard, cut timber, mechanic, operated the store, worked at Fairchild and lastly became Postmaster at Flintstone in 1957. Although I could write a book on the things my parents did during their lives, that isn't why I am writing but it is an important part of my story. It's part of who I am.

My Story

I understand there will be those who will question some of the things I write and will try to explain them away or totally reject my words as being just my imagination or the pizza I had the night before. To put it quite bluntly there will be those who question my integrity. Somehow I wish I could show them or let them experience what I have experienced but that isn't within my ability or purpose. The only thing I can do is tell my story to the best of my ability and pray the Holy Spirit can speak to you through my words.

Early in my life certain things stuck in my memory. When I was about two years old I remember a meteor or comet we watched from our living room window. The sound of a gentle summer breeze blowing through the big White Pines behind our house. There isn't another sound as whisper soft, but why did I remember a sound?

When I was about 9 or 10, I remember Mom and Dad reading the Bible and discussing the Book of Revelation, the beast and events of the Last Days. I have to say it was scary for a young boy who didn't understand.

Sometime during my younger years, something happened that would come back to me years later, in a miraculous way.

I repeatedly had the same dream for weeks or months. I can't say exactly at what age this happened or how many times I had the dream. It was something I had totally forgotten but would come back in a course of events that I'll elaborate on later.

My Younger Years

What can I say; I believe my generation grew up in probably one of the best of times and I am sure other generations would say the same thing. I was a war baby, the war was over and growth in the economy was slow but steady. Technology was growing by leaps and bounds giving families more leisure time and life on the farm was no longer the primary way of life. Many people were leaving the rural homestead and moving to urban and metropolitan homes following new progress of industry and better-paying jobs.

Soon after the war Mom and Dad built a house on the hill just south of Flintstone. I can remember walking around the newly laid block foundation with my Mom thinking this was a very strange thing as it stuck in my memory. I was only about two years old. During this time Dad went to trade school to be a mechanic and worked at several garages in Cumberland.

When I was two or three years old Dad went to Canton, Ohio looking for work and Mom and I followed shortly thereafter. It's funny how certain things stick in your memory even at this very young age. The trip to Ohio is in my memory like it happened yesterday, the apartment we lived in over the ice cream shop, the busy street in front of the house, the park across the street.

I remember the day we went to the amusement park and were in a car accident, a fender bender. For some reason, I wouldn't talk for some time after but I do remember the ride home that afternoon just like it was yesterday.

After some time Dad went to Baltimore following work and for me some memories while living in Baltimore. Calamine Lotion, for the hives I had from drinking the water. My cousin Wilma and I running up and down the stairs leaving our crayon marks on the stair walls. My mother and Aunt Betty were not too happy when they had to scrub them off. I remember building a nice fire in the drain of the alley behind the apartment building. I got quite a talking to over that one.

I guess the old saying is true, "You can take the boy out of the country but you can't take the country out of the boy." For after about a year or so we were moving back to Flintstone. Mom and Dad bought the store my grandfather built in 1937 and later sold to Mr. Musgrove.

Seems that Mr. Musgrove didn't have a clear deed to the property as my Grandfather wouldn't allow my Grandmother to sign the deed. Thinking that my Grandfather would give his son a clear deed, Mr. Musgrove sold the store to my Dad, Wrong! Dad never got a clear deed until after my Grandfather died.

My Grandfather was a very shrewd businessman, after the death of my Dad I had the privilege, or should I say the task of going through the boxes of papers that were left in the home place. The family didn't throw much of anything away, now I know where I get it from! Boxes of business receipts, letters, deeds and ledger books, gave me a history of my family I never knew existed. My grandfather went to college and was a college professor. Later he went back to college so he could teach high school at Flintstone and a school in Pennsylvania.

During his younger years, my grandfather served in the Medical Corp during the First World War as he claimed exemption from fighting as a member of the Brethren Church. At one time he even considered becoming a pastor, maybe because his father was a pastor, but for some reason he gave it up.

Growing up in Flintstone

G rowing up in Flintstone was an adventure for a young boy. With my best friend Bobby we explored all the streams, built dams and went fishing whenever the thought crossed our minds. We spent hours watching Eddie Wigfield in his blacksmith shop, it was a boy's dream world. When we weren't roaming over the countryside we were building huts on the hill, setting box traps for rabbits or trying to smoke squirrels out of hollow oak trees.

Life was good for two boys who were out to try most anything that came along. I'm sure if we grew up in today's world we probably would have been locked up for some of the things we got into.

School Years

Now school was a different thing; I started the first grade in 1952, the year my brother Greg was born. I remember getting set in the corner in the first grade, for some reason? I really don't remember why, probably because I talked too much. I didn't like school, the best part of school was summer vacation, and the last two weeks before school started in the fall was awful! The anticipation of going back to school just ate at me inside, not the way to end a summer!

Boy Scouts became a big part of my growing up; I was active in Scouting until I graduated from High School. It wasn't until Junior High did things change. Sports, especially Soccer, FFA and Girls made life tolerable, probably not in that order! With the distractions from schoolwork, school became a little more interesting, but the grades didn't improve much. I wasn't a bad student I just didn't like school. It wasn't interesting.

Somewhere during my Junior and Senior year I started thinking of a career in Electronics. In my younger years I was always tearing old radio's and anything electrical apart, even fixing a few. I'm sure my Dad had some influence in this as during his time in the store and later he was doing TV repairs and installing antennas for people in the Flintstone area. I'm pretty sure we were one of the very first families to have a TV in the area.

Dad had a TV in the store and I can remember people gathering around the potbelly stove to watch TV, some for the very first time.

I remember Hughs Imes, he was a somewhat recluse who lived in a small cabin along Flintstone Creek across from my grandparents. He would come to the store almost every day to have a Coca-Cola with a Stanback, (for those younger, Stanback was a type of pain medicine something like aspirin but in a powder form) and he would sit for hours watching the TV before walking back home.

It was decided I would go to Electronics School instead of college. I guess to a certain extent college scared me as it reminded me too much of High School and I thought a Trade School would be different.

October 1964 I moved to Pittsburgh and started school at Electronics Institute. Talk about a radical change in life! I moved into a boarding house with about 10 other students. I was on the third floor with five students and it wasn't long before I was doing most of the cooking, As I didn't like to wash dishes I left the dish washing to the others. When we ran out of clean dishes I stopped cooking. It was interesting when Mom and Dad came for a visit and the sink was stacked high with dirty dishes which had been there for over a week. Let's just say Mom wasn't too impressed!

I never liked Pittsburgh. For some reason it was like the end of the world and after about four months we found another Electronics school in Baltimore, Maryland. Looking back, this was my first time away from home which probably had a lot to do with my dislike of Pittsburgh.

Moving to Baltimore, again I found myself living in a boarding house with other students. After a few weeks I found out one of my High School classmates was living in Baltimore and we made arrangements to get together.

This would change everything as it gave me a connection with home, someone I knew and could do things with. Terry and I were good friends in High School and played soccer on the school team.

Terry lived in an apartment on Park Avenue which belonged to his sister's husband. As it was Terry lived alone and it wasn't too long before I moved in. This worked out well for me as it was much closer to my school and I could walk to school instead of riding a Transit Bus for forty-five minutes. It wasn't too long before Rich and Skip from school moved in also.

Radio Electronics Television School, (R.E.T.S.) was located on the Inner Harbor of Baltimore across the street from Conley's Restaurants and the pier where the Revolutionary War ship, Constellation, was docked. This was an interesting time. School was going great and my journey to school every day went through "The Block", that was an education in itself but not one you wrote home about!

In the evening after school, I worked at State Sales and Service with Frank Dinato, I worked on Juke Boxes, Pin Ball Machines and installed background music systems in some of the very best restaurants in the Baltimore area. One of the best benefits of this job was after hours of running wires and installing speakers, some of the restaurant owners would treat us to dinner, I can still remember several of the Jewish Restaurants in Reisterstown and the great food we had!

Over the next year our apartment became a stopping off point for many of our friends and classmates, some on their way to joining the Military and on to Viet Nam. Some went to work at Martin's in the machine shop.

A Winter Storm

During the winter of 1965-66, we had one of the biggest snowstorms I can remember. Highways were closed and we had snowdrifts 40 feet high. As it happened I was home in Flintstone when the snowstorm hit and couldn't go back to Baltimore. With not much else to do, many of my friends and old school mates got together at Kolb's house to play cards and ping pong. Larry Kolb was the Ping Pong champ to beat! Kolb's house had always been a gathering place when we were in High School.

As fate would have it, I walked Bonnie home later that evening. She lived on Merley's Branch Road on the south side of Flintstone about a half mile away. This was to be a turning point in our lives. Although we knew each other most all our lives, there had been no attraction until that night. Bonnie was going to Frostburg State Teachers College and I was in Baltimore. As we walked the snowy road that wintry night we talked about our hopes and dreams for the future, finding many common interest and goals. After returning to school I started coming home almost every weekend to see Bonnie and our relationship became more serious.

On one particular Sunday evening before returning to Baltimore, Bonnie and I were walking up the road to her home. I guess I was showing off a little too much. We were racing but I was running backward. I was quite good at it and was keeping up with her until losing my footing and fell on my tail bone. Off to the hospital, X-rays' and a shot. I don't know what the shot was but I was still feeling the effects of it the next day when I took a test for AT&T.

The test had four parts and you had to pass each part to go on to the next one, after the first three parts I was the only person taking the last section. I always believed the shot kept me calm during the test, so out of my whole class I was the only person offered employment at AT&T. I didn't take the job, I didn't want to move to Washington, DC.

As it was, I had 5 different job offers and was to start each one on the same day. Westinghouse, National Cash Register, Western Union, AT&T, and Bendix Radio. I went to work at Bendix, maybe not the best choice of companies but it was the closest.

As I finished school and was beginning my years of employment, Terry joined the Air Force, Donnie joined the Marines and I moved to Ruxton which was closer to Bendix Radio in Towson.

Even with the new job, I knew the Draft was just around the corner. I was losing my "2S" status as a student. Now being re-classed "1A" I was thinking I would work the summer of 1966 and join the Air Force in September before I would be drafted. It was just a matter of time!

When I started working I bought Bonnie an engagement ring. This triggered a series of ups and downs in our relationship. Bonnie was dealing with commitment and, as her mother had taught her, marriage was for a lifetime. Over the next year, we were engaged three times, but something kept us together.

On Sunday, August 28, 1966, I was coming back from Chaneysville to pick her up to go swimming at Van Meter's Beach. I was involved in a car accident which left me semi-unconscious for three days and I had double vision for several months.

The question kept wandering around in my mind. "Why wasn't I killed?" Looking back on these events I could see where it was not in God's plan for me to go into the military and Viet Nam. Most all of my family was Air Force and I wanted to follow in my Dad's footsteps, but it wasn't to be!

Bonnie would be by my side most of the time during this ordeal. Then she went back to college at Frostburg and our relationship started going downhill again. Then her lung collapsed and she dropped out of college.

Although we never severed our relationship, it was pretty rocky until she told me she was pregnant and she had to make a life-changing decision. Was she going to marry me? As the course of events happened I knew this was to be, this was no accident! Although I didn't understand the concept of Divine Intervention, I knew this was the person I was to share the rest of my life with and some things were in play beyond my understanding.

A New Life

We were married on Saturday, June 3, 1967, in the United Methodist Church across the road from my home. This was Bonnie's home church. The talk in town was it would never last a year. What can I say fifty-some years later? Something changed that day as our lives became one. We left Flintstone that night to start our life together. We moved into a small apartment I found on Old Eastern Avenue and I was back to work on Monday morning.

We didn't go on a Honeymoon until three weeks later when we went to Niagara Falls and north in Canada to Algonquian Provincial Park for a week on one hundred twenty dollars. Our parents thought it was terrible that it was all the money we had, but we had each other which was enough!

I was soon to find out I was being used by my supervisor at Bendix to get a promotion, telling me I was being considered for the job. I had made some changes to the wiring harness of a unit we were building. Previously the unit was destroyed in testing and I had come up with a new way to secure the wiring harness, which he took credit for.

Most of the projects I worked on during my career in electronics were related to the military and the war in Viet Nam. The job market in Electronics was wide open during the Sixties.

Through the employee grapevine, I heard about a job as a Job Shopper at Fairchild Hiller in Germantown, Maryland, this was something new for me but the money looked good. I would be working for a company called Lehigh Design Company and hired out to Fairchild.

After driving back and forth for a week or two with several other guys, Bonnie and I found an apartment in Gaithersburg which was only fifteen minutes away from work. I had been working at Fairchild for several months when I was offered a full-time job with Fairchild, as my contractual job was coming to an end. This worked out perfectly as it gave us insurance to pay for Robby when he was born several months later on January 7, 1968. Most insurance companies would not pay under such a short enrollment.

Next Gretchen was born March 6, 1969. Now with a family, we started considering if this was where we wanted to live and raise a family. What took me 15 minutes to drive to work, now was taking me 35 to 40 minutes two years later. Montgomery County was growing by leaps and bounds. Gaithersburg was becoming congested with traffic and no longer the nice country town we had known.

While at Fairchild I worked primarily on radar systems and one top-secret project for the Air Force. It seemed that when something was done wrong by someone else I was the one they called to fix it. Several times on a Ground Weather Radar System for the Army a rewiring had to be made. The console for the system was fired up one weekend by the Engineers before it was checked out and they blew it up. I was called into the office on Monday morning and asked if I would fix it. Given two weeks I was able to rewire it in a little over a week.

Then the trailer for the Radar System was wired wrong, all the separate modules for the radar system plugged into a main wiring harness of the trailer. I had to go over every connector, hours and hours of tracing wires.

During this project we had a visit by the Army. It seems when the Army comes everything is cleaned to the Max, I guess to impress them. After cleaning up all my tools and the trailer inside and out, I was trying to figure out why one of the interlocks wasn't working. Losing track of time I soon had the schematics out on the floor of the trailer with some of my tools, when two Generals and several of our Engineers were standing in the doorway of the trailer looking in.

If the looks I was getting from one of the Engineers could have killed, I would have been dead for having things on the floor. Then one of the Generals said; "Looks like this is the only place anyone is doing any work." Let's just say I could have been looking for another job!

While working on a Top Secret project I spent months working on the Antenna Test Range. I could come and go pretty much as I pleased as the test range was outside of the main facility. It was always fun when a supervisor would ask me what I was doing and I could say, "Can't tell you. It's Top Secret." Little did they know I was probably goofing off.

Two of my best friends at Fairchild were Hubert Weaver and Steve Lipowitz. Between the three of us there wasn't much of anything at Fairchild we didn't know where it was or how to get something done. Hubert was our Soul Brother, Steve was our Hebrew Brother and I was known as the Blue-Eyed Soul Brother, the Three Amigos of a higher order.

About the same time, Fairchild was gearing up to bid on a Satellite contract and I didn't feel comfortable with what I was seeing. They were hiring hundreds of new employees.

In the interim, I had found a job at National Jet Co. in LaVale, Maryland and we moved back home into a house across from the school in Flintstone. I found out later Fairchild lost the contract, but then several months later the contract was re-awarded to them. Politics!.

This job at National Jet was to be short-lived for after a few months I could see this job was dead-ended and I started looking for another place of employment. Somehow Mr. Cupler, owner and founder of the company, found out that I was looking for another job and laid me off.

A Change in Occupation

After being out of work for a couple of months I started working for Hazelwood Construction Company. I would have started earlier but the Union members were on strike for higher wages, I wasn't complaining but I remember wondering how this would affect the economy?

Bonnie had gone back to work at Sears part-time as a Cashier. She had worked there for a brief time before we got married. This helped with our finances until I went back to work.

I started as a Rod and Chainman on the Survey Crew in the summer of 1970. This was a learning experience. Fortunately, I had a great teacher, Willard Greene was the Project Engineer and a very good instructor. When he was writing field notes I was leaning over his shoulder taking in everything he did and when I didn't understand what he was doing he would explain the process.

Another little twist; the math and trigonometry I learned and used for electronics was the same as used in survey work. Instead of plotting a power graph we were now laying out curves in the road.

The stories I could tell of the years I worked for Hazelwood; building roads, bridges, buildings and yes even trying to build a road in the middle of a hurricane. I will spare you the torture of all the stories, except for one.

As you know on a construction job you will always see everyone wearing a hard hat. Even out in the middle of a field you had to have a hard hat on. I guess it is to protect you from falling parts from airplanes or a falling meteor. At the time, we were building three bridges; one in LaVale, one over old Route 36 south of Frostburg and one over

Midlothian road. I loved building bridges. It was more challenging because everything was more precise. With road work, you laid it out to the hundredth of a foot and if it ended up within one or two inches it was okay. Bridges had to be held to the hundredth of a foot. These measurements were so critical the temperature had to be known to compensate for the expansion and contraction of the steel tape measure.

As the projects progressed the steel beams were set on the bridge in LaVale and it was our job to run grades/ elevations on the beams every twenty-five feet. Now, this doesn't sound too challenging until you take into consideration that these beams had rows of six-inch top hat studs about twelve inches apart covering the top of the beam, for the concrete to attach to. When you walked the beam you had to walk between the studs and if you didn't tie your pants legs they would get caught on the studs, not a good thing!

To make it more interesting you are carrying the level rod, spray paint, marker pen, three-foot level, six foot folding rule, plumb-bob and the chain, (if you don't know what a chain is, it's a steel tape measure one hundred feet long). Oh, and you didn't want to forget your hard hat, just in case you fell off the bridge and landed on your head in the middle of the traffic below.

As this was my first bridge to work on, I had spent maybe an hour or so on the steel beams.

Several days later we were working on the bridge over Midlothian Road and I was out on the steel and Willard was on the West end of the bridge when an OSHA inspector drove up behind him. I was in the middle of the bridge while they were talking when I realized I didn't have my Hard Hat on. Oh my, this isn't going to be good! After about ten minutes, the inspector drove away and I worked my way back to where Willard was standing by the transit.

As I came off the steel beam I asked, "What did that cost us?"; As the Company could be fined for me not having my hard hat on, Willard grinned and said, "He wanted to know if you were an experienced bridge walker." We had a good laugh over that one. With a couple of hours on the steel, I was an "Experienced Bridge Walker," I now had a new title to add to my resume.

An Encounter with God

Sometime during the summer of 1971, we were attending Glendale Church of the Brethren. Several years earlier Pastor Buffenmeyer had died and we were going through a series of candidates for a new pastor. Terrell Mallow was speaking on this particular Sunday morning and I was half paying attention to his message when he gave an altar call. I can't explain what happened but something was drawing me forward to receive Christ. It was as if I wasn't in control. All I knew I had to go forward.

I remember him praying with me and I went back to my seat. After the service, not one person came up to me except Mary Teter. She was the only person who seemed to care or show any sign of encouragement for my new life as a Christian.

As it came to be after months or a year, I went back to my old ways. I can't say what really happened as I didn't have any guidance to help me with my spiritual experience or what I should do next. Being a new Christian without spiritual guidance is difficult. But God had a plan!

Where to Next

A fter several years of working for Hazelwood, I moved on to another
job with L. G. DeFlease from North Haven, Conn.. Hired as the
Instrument man on the Survey Crew. This was a move up as I was now
on salary and not a part of the Union. This project became known as
the Jennings Randolph Dam or Lake and we were building the water
control tunnel through the mountain on the West Virginia side of the
dam. After several months, I became the Crew Chief running my first
survey crew.

Survey work was both challenging and rewarding to see a project
come together. Everything on a construction project depended upon
the work of the Survey Crew and when you are leading the Survey Crew
it all falls on your shoulders. Mistakes were not an option!

While on this project, I saw an Ad in the Cumberland Newspaper
where a company was looking for Electronic Technicians to start a new
company in Cumberland. Although I was only going to see who and
what they were offering. I didn't think they would be paying what I
would need. One evening after work I stopped in Cumberland to meet
with a Mr. Shapiro of Microdyne Corp. After a lengthy discussion,
Mr. Shapiro said he would get back to me in a couple of weeks when
they would be making their final decisions. I left that meeting with no
expectations and went on with business as usual. Several weeks came
and went and to be truthful, I didn't think much about it.

On a Sunday evening after returning from the Zoo in Washington
D.C. I received a phone call from Mr. Shapiro. He apologized for not
getting back to me sooner saying, "You probably didn't think you were
going to hear from me."(No I didn't!) He went on to say they were
having problems with different aspects of the move, permits and a

building. Then he asked me how I would like to be the manager. I was a little stunned and just listened to what he had to say. He wanted me to start in four weeks and I would spend my first two weeks at their facility in Rockville, Md.

After accepting the job offer, I went back to work the next day and told them I would be leaving in four weeks so they could find someone to replace me. Not wanting to put them on a spot trying to find someone in two weeks.

This didn't work like I thought it would, as the project engineer didn't talk to me for two weeks. A little difficult to say the least!
After two weeks Jon came to me and apologized, saying he had wanted me to run several bridge projects in Garrett County on the new Interstate 68, but he understood why I would want a job closer to home.

Microdyne Corporation was another new experience and after spending two weeks in Rockville, I came back to Cumberland for the construction of an Electronics Lab. Starting with a total makeover of the old bakery on Henderson Ave. into a working Electronics Lab was challenging. Then came the hiring of Lab Techs and Quality Control Inspectors.

Now with thirty-two women and six men, we started building components for Satellite Communications Equipment. Dealing with employee issues and meeting schedules, things were going well, life was good.

After about nine months at Microdyne, I received a notice in the mail that Maryland Park Service was hiring 11 new Rangers. I had previously interviewed for a Ranger position at Assateague Island State Park, but I didn't get the job. With this new recruitment campaign, I put in an application and waited for the test. State tests are always fun with all multiple-choice questions. With four possible answers to each question, two you could usually throw out right away and two were a tossup as to which was correct. I guess I usually chose right as I normally got in the nineties on most state tests.

Later I received a notice for interviews in Annapolis at the Maryland Park Service Headquarters. At the interview I met Dave Hathway who was Operations Director. The first thing he brought up was the interview for Assateague Island, telling me the only reason I didn't get the job was because the person who did, already worked for MPS giving him preference. Then he asked me if I knew where I was on the list? I said no, so he went on to tell me I was number two on the list of 800. Gary Durr wasn't number one on the list but he had worked for the State Highway Administration. Being a State employee gave him priority for the job at Rocky Gap State Park which was my first and only choice. Time to step back and regroup.

Mr. Hathway asked if I had considered any other parks. I told him I hadn't but would consider it. He said Mr. Sword from Point Lookout State Park was there and suggested I talk to him and I could stop at Green Brier State Park on the way home and talk with Curtis Conway.

Where was Point Lookout?

Choices or God's Direction

Point Lookout

After talking to Gerry Sword about Point Lookout, I stopped at Greenbrier State Park on the way home. Mr. Conway seemed very enthused about me starting before Memorial Day weekend but he would give me a call before the weekend and let me know definitely when to start. After not hearing from Mr. Conway, I figured I would call Gerry Sword at Point Lookout to look at the park, so we made plans to go camping at Point Lookout the next weekend.

Sometime later I found out Mr. Sword had called Mr. Conway and asked him not to hire me as he wanted me at Point Lookout.

After going for a tour of the park we were taken to the Point Lookout Lighthouse as a possible place of residence. The lighthouse was built in 1836 and the residences were added later.

Bonnie was a firm "No" on the lighthouse as the water was only 20 to 30 feet from the lighthouse on two sides, not a place to raise three children!

Mr. Sword then took us to St. Mary's River State Park and a nice house in the woods. St Mary's was an undeveloped park several miles west of Lexington Park, Maryland, so I accepted the position.

Several days later I received a phone call from Mr. Sword stating the rent on the house offered to us was going to triple. I turned the job down as we couldn't afford the rent. A short time later another house was offered which was in the middle of Point Lookout across from the Old Hotel. Although I can't remember the exact details or timing of events, I turned the offer down again.

A few days later Bonnie and I were talking by phone, during our conversation it turned to the Ranger job at Point Lookout and the housing situation. Here is where things took a different turn. Unexpected and out of the norm an unknown peace came over us and at the same time we each said and agreed to take the job and move to Point Lookout.

This would start a chain of events that would change our lives, although we never gave it any thought at the time. As the old saying goes, "hindsight is always twenty-twenty." Now looking back we can see how God was directing events unknown to us. Now for anyone who has never experienced anything like this, the explanation might be simple. It was just the luck of the draw or it just happened that way. I guess I would probably agree with the skeptics but as you look back at the series of events and choices that were placed before us I would have to change my opinion. Yes, one, two or even three events are maybe possible, but it didn't stop there.

While what I am writing can never change anyone's life and never will without God speaking. I can't tell you how many times I have shared my story and the person would say, "I have goosebumps all over me." I have wondered what makes one person react that way and another can't get away fast enough.

I cannot explain the operation of the Holy Spirit, it is something that has to be experienced. That goes for believers and non-believers alike. You will find those who will adamantly argue that the things of the Holy Spirit are not for today.

Some will only acknowledge some of the gifts of the Spirit and then others have no idea what I am talking about. I can only reiterate what the scriptures have to say and what I have experienced.   From that point on it is the responsibility of the Holy Spirit to speak to you.

The next day I called Mr. Sword to see if the position was still open and to go look at the house offered us. After everything was confirmed I gave my notice to Microdyne Corp, so the process started. We were moving!

During my last weeks with Microdyne, I had a meeting in Rockville and while there I ran into a guy I had worked with at Fairchild. Max had worked in the Calibration Lab and when he saw me he said, "You're just the guy I'm looking for." He asked, "How would you like to go to Australia for two years?" I replied, "Max, if you had asked me two weeks ago I would have jumped at it, but I had just accepted a Ranger job with Maryland Park Service."

I had previously looked into working on a Radar Tracking Station but nothing was available at the time except Madagascar and who wanted to go to Madagascar? If I knew then what I know now, things might have been different? Madagascar could have been interesting.

That same day I was in the hall at the coffee machine when the company president stopped by. We were talking when he said he had a lawsuit against the State of Maryland. I didn't understand what he was talking about? I asked him, "what for", I was a little puzzled? He said, "For taking one of my best employees!" It still didn't sink in, then it hit me, he was talking about me! He said, "You know you made money for us the first year and we didn't expect to. You know you had a nice pay raise coming to you." I said, "Don't tell me, I don't want to know." You see I was already taking a pay cut going to work for the State.

Looking back at these events I can now see how God will let events test you when He is directing your life, even when you don't know He is doing so. Satin will throw a nice juice bone out to try and draw you away from God's plan, if possible. As the old saying goes, "the grass always looks greener on the other side of the fence." Always follow the peace, "Always!" Satin can never give you peace, only turmoil and confusion.

It's a hard lesson to learn.

Life at the Point

Point Lookout! So much I could write, this was to be a big change in our lives. With three children and the new job, life would be a little different. Starting with Maryland Park Service on the 4th of July weekend was intense, but throw in a forest fire in the park that same weekend was insane!

Then that fall I started training; Ranger School, Maryland State Police Academy, a course in Archaeology at St. Mary's College, two weeks of Interpreter's training. Then Natural Resource Law, CPR, Coast Guard Boating Course and forty hours of First Aide, First Responders training rounded out most of the next year. This meant spending weeks away from the family, only coming home on weekends.

With most of the training behind me, it was time to settle down to the routine of Park life. I was soon to learn there is never a dull moment dealing with thousands of people in a park setting and settling down just does not happen. There wasn't much to call routine either!

I have to say, I had no idea what I was getting myself into when I first started pursuing a job as a Ranger. Living in the park comes with a new set of rules. You are on call 24 hours a day, lost children, stuck vehicles in the middle of the night, disturbances in the campground and medical emergencies, the list goes on.

Every park is unique and Point Lookout was no different, with the Civil War Prison Camp and Hospital, the Lighthouse, camping, picnic area, swimming, fishing, crabbing, and oystering. Point Lookout was exceptional!

Add to that the hurricanes, storms and the mosquitoes which could carry you off. Then there is the Causeway leading to the Point, with the Chesapeake Bay on one side and Lake Conoy on the other. The Causeway was about 60 feet wide and a great place to fish and crab. This was the only road to our home on the Point, but try driving this narrow stretch of road when the waves are breaking over the vehicle! Then Hurricane Agnes was another challenge when I had to drive the patrol sedan out from the Lighthouse with water inside the car up to the top of the seat. After wadding in I had to drive in reverse to not drown the engine.

We had moved to Point Lookout in June, 1974 and I started to work on the 3rd of July. Now that my training was over, it was adjustment time to a new way of life. Things were good.

We had more company, friends and family, who never came to see us at Flintstone. Now it seemed we were a destination, as we were on the Chesapeake Bay. Many times arriving unannounced, one time our company left and within an hour someone else arrived to stay two weeks, unannounced!

During the last year at the Point, I had put in for a transfer back to Rocky Gap. Knowing it was a long shot as everyone wanted to go West in the park system. The busy parks around the Bay were the training grounds for Park Service. From here many wanted to go to Western Maryland to the quieter parks. Once there, they retired there. So there weren't many opening in Western Maryland Parks.

Where is Calvert Cliffs

In the summer of 1976, I received a notice for an interview for Greenbrier State Park near Hagerstown, but I had not put in for a transfer to Greenbrier. I called Annapolis Headquarters to talk to Dave Hathway who was in charge of park operations. I told him there must have been a mistake as I hadn't put in for Greenbrier. Dave said to come on up for the interview so we could talk. What was this all about!?

A week or so later I went to the interview, still wondering what was going on. As a person had to put in for a transfer to interview, this was a little unusual, especially for a rather new Ranger. I had only been with the Department for a little more than two years.

At the interview Dave started with an apology for no position at Rocky Gap, he knew I had wanted to go back to my home in Flintstone. Then he asked me. "What about Greenbrier?" I told him I had no interest in Greenbrier and secondly, I couldn't afford to live in the Hagerstown area. Next came the shocker! "How would you like to go to Calvert Cliffs?" He went on to say that Richard Bowers was going to be offered the position of Assistant Manager of Elk Neck and they wanted someone to run Calvert Cliffs. He further stated that I would not be the Manager but I would be "Ranger in Charge". (In other words all the responsibility, but not the pay) Reporting to John Westerfield at Cedarville, I had known John for some time and was comfortable with that.

I was told I had until Monday to give him an answer, they hadn't talked to Richard yet. They were meeting with him on Monday as he was on vacation. I told Dave I didn't know anything about Calvert Cliffs. He said to arrange it and go check the park out.

The next day, Friday, I called to make arrangements, only to find out Richard came home early from vacation. So I was to meet him on Saturday.

Upon arriving at Calvert Cliffs, I met Richard and was asking him about the house he lived in and things about the park. I could tell by his reaction he was totally in the dark as to why I was there asking all these questions.

I then asked Richard if he had a meeting in Annapolis on Monday, he said yes, they had called him. I said, well they are going to offer you the Assistant's position at Elk Neck and I was there to take his place.

After touring the park and a lengthy conversation, I went back to Point Lookout and told Park Manager Jerry Sword that I was going to be moving to Calvert Cliffs. I had no idea Jerry didn't know about the job offer, he was very upset as he wasn't in the loop about what was going on?

I was soon to find out there were several Rangers who were also upset as they were never given a chance to interview for Calvert Cliffs. Including one Ranger I worked with at Point Lookout.

Two weeks later, we were moving into Calvert Cliffs just hours after Richard and his family had moved out. Life at Calvert Cliffs was different and interesting, so much to learn. Little did I know what lay ahead. For things were set in place as God's plans were again about to make changes in our lives.

Life was good, things were going great! Kids were all in school and Bonnie was involved with Cub Scouts and Blue Birds, but something was happening! I had the ideal job; things were going smoothly and I had no problems with work. But something I couldn't explain was going on within me.

At any time day or night I would have a fear of death come over me that would shake me to the bone. Nothing I could do would stop it, it would just come all of a sudden day or night. I saw my life as a speck in the midst of an endless darkness. I was lost and didn't know it. This went on for months; I would wake up in the middle of the night in a cold sweat for fear of dying. Nothing like this had ever happened to me before in my life. What was going on?

March 27, 1978

A God Encounter

Little did I know what was coming. For the past six or seven months I had been fighting this battle within myself, and let me tell you, I was not winning!

Easter weekend came and went. I had worked the weekend as I worked most weekends. Being the only Ranger there was only one other full-time employee, Griff would filled in for me when I needed a weekend off. This worked out pretty well. I didn't have to come up with an excuse for not going to church. Monday would be my day off in place of the holiday.

March 27th, Monday morning! About 6:30 a.m., the unthinkable, the unexpected happened, God spoke to me! In an instant, I have no idea how long it took, all I can say is when God speaks you don't have to wonder who is speaking, you know!

God said; "You either straighten your life out here and now or you never get another chance!"

I sat up in bed with the hair standing up on the back of my neck, tears coming down my cheeks. At that moment everything in my life was laid before Him. My life was never to be the same again and I knew it! There were things I had to do, people I had wronged that I had to go to and I had to ask my wife's forgiveness for things I had done to her. It was all in God's hands! I had surrendered to God!

In that instant, it was like someone opened up my head and dumped a whole book of knowledge into it. I knew the Bible was true and my life was in God's hands now. I didn't know what was coming next. I didn't have to worry, for the Creator of the Universe was now in charge!

Unknown to me, two weeks later our friends, Jack and Idella Edwards, were leading a Lay Witness Mission in our church at Saint Paul UMC.

What was a Lay Witness Mission?

My first real encounter with the LWM (Lay Witness Mission) was on Saturday morning at a church member's home. Over coffee and donuts, a group discussion was held on a series of questions. During this time one of the questions presented cut me to the core. It became one of the questions I was to use for many years after. It's interesting how one simple statement can change your whole way of thinking, the question was asked;

"If you were put on trial for being a Christian, could they find enough evidence to convict you?"

Now for me having gone through months of training of our laws and the legal use of evidence, it hit me as to how convicting evidence can be, if it's there! I knew the evidence wasn't there, a good person maybe yes but evidence of a Christian?

Life was different! The biggest noticeable change was that I could sleep as I had never slept before, sleep was so sound and peaceful. I couldn't get over the difference!

I began reading, mainly the Bible and any Christian books that I could get hold of. I went out and bought a King James Version of the Bible and will have to say I found it hard to read and somewhat out of touch with what just happened. God had spoken to me and I didn't have any trouble understanding Him. I was looking for something that spoke to me the same way. Wasn't this supposed to be the Word of God? Then it was suggested I look at the "New International Version" of the bible. Here I found a bible that spoke a language I could understand without trying to figure the meaning of the words, which were used hundreds of years ago. All of the Thee's and Thou's are not part of our vocabulary today and as far as I was concerned didn't make understanding any easier. I knew God didn't speak to me that way.

The next months were a training experience. I would get up every morning to spend time reading the bible and praying. I was like a sponge soaking up everything I could get. Little did I know I was searching for answers or that something that would put this all in perspective, to make it real! God speaking was as real as life can get, but it seemed there had to be more?

Later in the spring, we were preparing for a Tri-County 4H event in the Park. This was to be held in the "Old Girl Scout Camp" which was our Youth Group Area (Bay Breeze). While working on the roof of the Old Dining Hall,I stepped off a small porch onto the ground, no big thing! Little did I know there was a 2x4 block in the leaves, my right foot hit the side of the block and rolled my ankle, dislocated it and tore the ligaments. The pain was so great I couldn't say anything. I lay on the ground for several minutes not wanting to get Griff excited and him fall off the ladder.

I finally was able to call him and we were on our way to the hospital. After x-rays and a cast, we were on our way back to the park and home. When Bonnie saw me getting out of the truck on crutches she thought we were playing a prank on her. Not Me!

After two weeks off, I was back to work, in a cast and on crutches. I worked for six weeks with my leg in a cast, a learning experience. Working for the State had its advantages and disadvantages. They were willing to let me work with my leg in a cast (as they didn't have anyone to replace me.) But when it came to moving back to Western Maryland I lost four weeks Comp-time because the State wouldn't let me take it.

A Lesson Learned

God has a way of teaching us lessons we would never think of. I was asked to fill in and teach a Sunday School Class. Not wanting to look foolish in front of the class, I studied and had the lesson down pat, not a hard task! Sunday morning came and everyone started coming in and finding their seats for the class to begin, I was ready!

After starting with an opening prayer, I opened my notes and Sunday School Book. I looked around to each person sitting there, and then it happened! The unthinkable! I couldn't open my mouth, what was happening! I just sat there with this dumbfounded look on my face. What do you do when you can't talk and you are the teacher? It must have become obvious there was something wrong for Jack took over and taught the class. The Lord wouldn't let me open my mouth, I couldn't say a thing! Now I don't know if you understand what happened to me. It wasn't shock or new teacher jitters, I just couldn't open my mouth and talk, I was helpless to say anything. I had been in front of hundreds of people before, had to speak impromptu to a group of people who were my peers, so I was not out of my element.

Afterward, the light came on; the Lord was showing me a lesson as to who was in charge. See I was ready to teach the class but my confidence was in my ability. I hadn't prayed for the Lord's direction! This was a lesson learned the hard way.

The Search Is On

I find it amazing how we can be searching for something yet not know what we are looking for or even know we are searching!

As we come to find out our church family became our family. When you live in an area where most people are transplants, you come to socialize and depend on each other. We became close with five or six families, most had children the same age as our three and we did things together as most families do.

John and Elaine became our closest friends and we were back and forth having dinners or sharing the things of the Lord. During one of our visits, they began sharing things about the Holy Spirit. Although I had heard about the Holy Spirit most of my life, this was something new. As they talked about being baptized in the Holy Spirit and the gifts of the Spirit, I realized this was something I had never heard presented in this way. Spending most of my life in the church and hearing "Hell's Fire and Damnation", here was something that caught my attention. Was this the something I was looking for?

I grew up in the "Church of the Brethren" with people who lived in our small community and kids I went to school with. Our church was very conservative, simple country folks, many were relatives. My Great Grandfather was one of the first Pastors of this church in the early 1900s. Bonnie had attended the Methodist church across the road from where I lived in Flintstone and we had attended a Baptist church at Point Lookout.

As I was hearing this new teaching (new to me!) of the Holy Spirit I will have to say it stirred within me. I couldn't let it go; I had to know more about the Holy Spirit. I read and reread all the scriptures I could find related to the Holy Spirit and the gifts of the Spirit. Was this for me? I found and was given numerous books written on the subject. Everything I read seemed to confirm that this could be what I was seeking?

As the scriptures speak of being baptized in the Holy Spirit. I had to think about my water baptism in Flintstone Creek when I was 17 years old. Although it was more of a ritual thing as my mother insisted that I be baptized before I went off into the world. I would soon be going to school in Pittsburgh. Being from the Church of the Brethren and similar in teaching with the United Methodist Church. I had no teaching of the Baptism of the Spirit and everyone I talked to seemed to have a slightly different experience.

Over the next several months I continued my search, reading, talking to anyone who had experienced the Holy Spirit and went to many different churches that advocated the Baptism of the Holy Spirit. I was prayed for and had the laying on of hands more times than I could remember but nothing seemed to happen! I was somewhat confused and apprehensive as to what I was seeking. Was this for me?

An Appointment with the Holy Spirit

We had been planning a trip to Annapolis to do some Christmas Shopping. Early that morning I awakened and something strange was going on. I had something stirring inside of me. I got up and started reading my bible but I couldn't shake this uneasiness or excitement. I just couldn't explain it. This just wasn't like me or anything I had experienced. Everything was fine except there was something just hidden out of sight that I couldn't put my finger on. It was beyond my control or understanding.

Later as we were getting ready to leave I told Bonnie she would have to drive because I couldn't! The stirring that was going on inside of me left me uneasy as to my capability to drive. I knew I couldn't drive but there wasn't anything wrong with me! What was going on?

On our way to Annapolis, we were talking and listening to the radio. I will never forget it was WABC out of Baltimore, Md. The person on the radio was talking about tears. As we were listening something was happening in me but I don't know how to explain it, I couldn't control it!

I started to tell Bonnie if he didn't stop talking about tears, I was going to start crying. I never got the words out of my mouth when I started crying and laughing at the same time.

It was like something exploded inside of me, it just kept coming! It was pure joy, a release, a cleansing within. The only thing I will say is you have to experience it. It is freedom like you have never experienced before, nothing in this world can compare with it!

Now I understood the Baptism of the Holy Spirit, for God had sovereignly baptized me with his Spirit. Now I understood what happened in Acts, chapter two! God had set the world on fire by his Spirit. Every time I thought I had it under control, it would start all over again. This went on for some time and when we arrived in Annapolis, it was like I was in another world. The whole time we were shopping, it felt like I was walking three feet off the floor.

What Next!

That evening I called John and Elaine to tell them what happened and later they came over to our house. After talking some length about my experience, John was telling me about a series of tapes he had listened to concerning Judgment on the United States and the two men who recorded a total of seven cassette tapes. This was somewhat concerning, something I didn't want to believe but yet there was something within me that kept saying, "What if it is true?" I kept thinking, is there something to this, or was it just me?

Over the next several days I listened to all seven tapes, I couldn't stop listening, Was this real? I was in turmoil, not knowing just what to believe or explain what I was feeling.

Late one evening I went outside to walk around and think. I stopped by the side of the van and prayed, "Lord if this is of you. I want to know it but if it isn't you, I want to forget it and get on with my life." A very simple prayer, little did I know.

The next morning as I was waking up thinking, "What will I read this morning?" At that moments God spoke! "Read Ezekiel 14.", What! What was this? I had no question as to who spoke, but what was Ezekiel 14? I had been reading the Bible for some months but mostly the New Testament. I didn't even know where to find Ezekiel, let alone what it might say. I got up and went out to my desk and sat down. I opened my Bible to the table of contents to find Ezekiel. After several minutes I was reading chapter 14 of Ezekiel, as I was reading nothing spoke to me. It seemed totally foreign and I couldn't understand what God was trying to say.   Was I missing something?

I kind of backed up and looked at the whole page for some reason and that's when it happened! As I glanced down over the page, two words circled in fire just lifted off the page, **"Judgment Inescapable"**. At that moment you could have knocked me over with a feather. I was in shock. God had answered my simple prayer.

The next thing to weigh on me was the parts of the prophecy speaking of an invasion and struggles dealing with the occupation of an enemy force. Here we were located about five miles from Patuxent Naval Air Station and deep water Submarine Base. And to make things worse there is a Nuclear Power Plant on the north side of the Park and Colombia Gas LNG Terminal on the South side of the Park. If these things were true, this wasn't the best place to be when judgment came!

Again that night I went outside and prayed, again a very simple prayer; "Lord, are we going to be here or are you going to move us?" I didn't think much more about the prayer and went to bed. The next morning was like any other morning, except as I awakened the Lord again spoke to me, "Read Deuteronomy 1: 24", another scripture? I can't explain what it means or the feelings that stir within a person when God speaks.

Being new to this kind of Christianity or should I say, God, speaking to me! I didn't know what to expect I was not prepared for this kind of an encounter. I soon was in the book of Deuteronomy, chapter 1, verse 24, said, "And they went into the Hill Country…" Immediately the thought came to me of the mountains or hill of Flintstone. I knew the Holy Spirit had put these thoughts in my spirit but I wasn't sure what it all meant or was it just my imagination? You know but then there are the questions!

Relent

Now I know there are going to be those who have questions concerning "Judgment on America." Now some 50 years later that had to be a false prophet and prophecies? I wish I could say you are right!

Let's take a look at what the Bible has to say concerning prophecies of judgment. Particularly the word "Relent" and what it means. This word appears 22 times in the Old Testament.

Jeremiah 18:8
8 and if that nation I warned repents of its evil, then I will <u>relent</u> and not inflict on it the disaster I had planned.

Jeremiah 26:3
3 Perhaps they will listen and each will turn from their evil ways. Then I will <u>relent</u> and not inflict on them the disaster I was planning because of the evil they have done.

Jeremiah 26:13
13 Now reform your ways and your actions and obey the LORD your God. Then the LORD will <u>relent</u> and not bring the disaster he has pronounced against you.

Jeremiah 26:19
19 "Did Hezekiah king of Judah or anyone else in Judah put him to death? Did not Hezekiah fear the LORD and seek his favor? And did not the LORD <u>relent</u>, so that he did not bring the disaster he pronounced against them? We are about to bring a terrible disaster on ourselves!"

Ezekiel 24:14

14 " 'I the LORD have spoken. The time has come for me to act. I will not hold back; I will not have pity, nor will I <u>relent</u>. You will be judged according to your conduct and your actions, declares the Sovereign LORD.' "

Jonah 3:9

9 Who knows? God may yet <u>relent</u> and with compassion turn from his fierce anger so that we will not perish."

A simple definition of "Relent" means God changed his mind to show his mercy or postponed his Judgments.

Now here is my understanding or interpretation of what happened in 1979. This word went around the world and touched many lives, and I can attest, I was one of them. God spoke to me three times concerning judgment. I met this Prophet and held his staff. The power I felt in that staff was something I can not explain nor will I ever forget. I will say this about the prophecy... people prayed, many people prayed! Some of the events that were prophesied did happen, but in a much lessened magnitude. God relented!

So where do we stand today concerning Judgment, the warning signs are all around us if we will only open our eyes. God's Word will never come back void! As a nation I believe we are in great pearl, we are walking further and further away from God. The real question is what will be the straw that breaks the camels back? If it were not for the prayers of a Godly people I believe judgment would already be upon us. The warning signs are there. It is all in God's timing!

2 Chronicles 7:14

14 if my people, who are called by my name, will humble themselves and pray and seek my face and turn from their wicked ways, then I will hear from heaven, and I will forgive their sin and will heal their land.

Being Saturday morning I thought I would call our Pastor, John Williams, but when I called he wasn't home. I thought, oh well... I'll see him Sunday morning in church but when we got to church I found out John was off preaching at another church, so I was left with contacting him on Monday.

Monday morning I called the church and John answered the phone, I asked if he was busy and if I could come and talk to him. He said he was in a meeting and he would be finished in a little while, he would meet me in the fellowship hall of the church. Shortly after arriving at the church, John came in. We sat down and I started telling him what had happened over the past several days, I wasn't too sure how he would receive this or what he would have to say in response? John listened as I talked and when I finished, he said, "That just confirmed some things for me".

After talking for some time, I went back to the Park Office (which was in our home) with the intent of writing a letter of Request for Transfer. As I sat down at the typewriter to type the request I didn't know to whom I was to address the letter, so I called John Westerfield at Cedarville. John answered the phone and I told him I was writing a request for transfer and who was I to send it to? John said I should send it to Rusty Russin, and, by the way, Rusty is in the picnic area at Calvert Cliffs. He is looking for you!

I quickly typed Rusty's name into the letter, put it in an envelope, went to my truck, put the letter on the dash and drove the two and a half miles to the picnic area.

Rusty was sitting in his car when I arrived; I got out of the truck and walked over to his car as he was getting out. As we shook hands I ask him what he was doing at Calvert Cliffs?

(Calvert Cliffs was an undeveloped area and not on the way to any other park, so no one just stopped by Calvert Cliffs. So it was highly unusual for someone from Annapolis to come to this park)

Rusty said, "I am looking for something.", I didn't say a thing, went to the truck pulled the letter off the dash and handed it to him. Rusty opened the request for transfer, read it and said; "This is what I am looking for." We talked for a little while and I told him some of the things that had happened to me. He further stated that there were no openings at this time as there was a job freeze in effect. This was a statewide freeze for all state employees.

As Rusty drove away and I headed back to our house I couldn't believe what had just happened. The fact that I couldn't talk to John Williams until that Monday, just an hour before Rusty being there as I was writing the letter of transfer and it was what he was looking for. Are you kidding me!

A License Plate

Did you ever consider the possibilities of God speaking to you and I know some have had it happen. But to go a step further; how many different ways is it possible for Him to speak? I will make one comment. Don't Put God in a box! Never limit God! Keep an open mind, think of this, God created the whole universe and everything in it, with that given, He can do whatever He wants, any way He wants!

Sometime later I was driving back to the Park, a very nice winter day in Southern Maryland, sunny and warm for the season. Not thinking much of anything, when I noticed the license plate on the vehicle I was following, Maryland tag, "_ _ _599." As the number registered in my mind I knew it was a scripture. I have looked at and seen thousands of license plates and never had one speak to me as this one did. I knew!

Well, you may be thinking how do you know, what was different? The difference is the Holy Spirit and my experiences with the Holy Spirit. From the times God spoke to me there is something different, there is a knowing. It isn't something you can think up or contrive yourself. It never works that way.

When I got home I opened my Bible to the Old Testament, the fifth book of the Old Testament, let's see Genesis, Exodus, Leviticus, Numbers and then number five, Deuteronomy! I opened to chapter nine, verse nine, here is what it says;

"When I went up on the mountain to receive the tablets of stone, the tablets of the covenant that the Lord had made with you, I stayed on the mountain forty days and forty nights; I ate no bread and drank no water."

As I read the verse the last statement stood out to me; "I ate no bread and drank no water." Don't eat or drink for forty days? (Now understand without divine intervention this is impossible.) I knew I couldn't do that and I didn't know if I understood what the Lord was trying to tell me. So many times as you hear what God speaks to you, you are trying to understand or second guess what it means. Being new at this I thought, let's go to the New Testament and see what it has to say?

I opened to the New Testament, Mathew, Mark, Luke, John, and Acts was book number five, then on to chapter nine, verse nine, what was this going to say?

> "For three days he was blind, and did
> not eat or drink anything."

I couldn't believe what I was reading, another verse talking about fasting. Did God want me to fast? I knew He did. It couldn't have been clearer, but I was no martyr. I couldn't do forty days without food or water. Moses did it but I wasn't Moses. I'll take the three days as I had never fasted before.

The next question was when? Now as I said before; the scripture in Deuteronomy 1: 24 said, "And they went into the hill country." Although I had the witness of the hills of Allegany County in Western Maryland, I still needed to test the spirit as to my uncertainty and inexperience.

Sometime within these months, our friend John Potts had been in contact with a lady in Virginia who purchased a large tract of land on the mountainside bordering the Skyline Drive. The story passed on to John was that the Lord told her to buy the property for His work.

John somehow was in communication with this woman and a meeting was set up to go meet her and look at the mountain property.

Because of my message from the Lord, we were invited to go to Virginia with the Potts family and Pastor John's family. As it was, I decided to start my fast three day before we were to leave for Virginia. Although I was told to fast, I had no idea why nor did I even question why. God said it so there was no reason to question. I finished the fast the evening before we were to leave and we had communion. The fast was quite uneventful. After three days without eating or drinking, I had some problems taking any food or water for several days, as I was told later three days was about the limit to go without water. I never thought of this as I knew this was God's direction.

The next day we were off to Virginia to meet Jeanie and see "Jeanie's Mountain" as we had labeled it. Jeanie had prepared a very nice dinner for us and was a very cordial hostess. As the afternoon went on without event, including anything being mentioned of the mountain property, which was why we were there. It was finally said we should drive up the mountain to take a look at the property.

A short time later we were in the vehicles finally headed to see why we were there. After a few minutes we stopped and got out of the cars and walked a short distance but no conversation about her vision or what Jeanie wanted from us or why we were there. After a short time I had this strong knowing we were not to be there, so I finally spoke up and said, "It looks like we are wasting our time here. Jeanie isn't ready to do anything with this property and doesn't want us here." I could see by her reaction she wasn't ready to involve anyone in her property and I could tell there was a consensus of everyone as I was the one to speak it out.

Jeanie was trying to get John to pastor the small church there and he did preach several times but didn't feel it was what he was to do.

With the events of the fast and trip to Virginia, it finally sunk in and I realized there was something different. I was experiencing something I had never encountered before. There was something unusual going on within me, a knowing! The scripture speaks of it in 1 Corinthians twelve where it speaks of the Spiritual Gifts of the Holy Spirit, particularly the gift of Discernment. I don't know exactly how to explain this but I knew things about people's motives and circumstances without anyone saying anything or if they weren't being truthful when they did speak. This is a gift I have learned to depend upon over the years.

Things seemed to settle down for a couple weeks without any more encounters with the Holy Spirit.

Prophetic Confirmation

One morning Elaine and Cathy came over to see Bonnie. Sometime later we sat down for a time of prayer. As we went around the circle with individual prayers, something was happening. I had this compelling to speak and what came out was in another language. I was speaking in tongues as explained in the Bible. My arms started to burn as I spoke and I could tell the Holy Spirit was doing something when Cathy started prophesying over me. The longer she spoke, the greater the power of the Holy Spirit became until I was laying on the floor under the power of the Holy Spirit. I couldn't get up!

As she continued, she spoke of the Gift of Healing and "that which wasn't the normal now would become the norm in days to come." It was days before the burning stopped in my arms and I knew God was speaking to me again about a time to come.

The Phone Call

Several days later we were watching TV in the evening when the telephone rang, I answered it. It was David Woodburn from Point Lookout. David was a young man from the Ridge, Maryland area who worked seasonally at the Park. David told me Jerry Denton had an accident and was burned severally at his new home when a gas can exploded in his basement and set the house on fire. Jerry was a Ranger and good friend who had just built a new home in Mechanicsville, Md.

I later learned Jerry was building a fire in the basement wood stove when he threw what he thought was diesel fuel on the fire, which turned out to be old gas and oil mixed for an outboard motor. Because the mixed gas was several years old it smelled like diesel fuel. When it hit the flames, it exploded setting the can on fire and the can exploded, burning his legs. As the flames spread it burned the wiring to the electric panel causing the water pump to shut off, leaving him without water to put the fire out. The flames spread to the floor joist melting the nylon mesh that held the insulation in place. The melted nylon dripped on his head, shoulders and ears as he tried to put the fire out.

David went on, "Can you go do something?" At first I was at a loss as to what I could do, but I told him I would go to the hospital to find out what I could.

I drove to Leonardtown arriving at the hospital to find Pat, Jerry's wife and children in the lobby as I entered the hospital. Pat filled me in with the details and was going over where everyone was going to stay that night. Plans were made for everyone except Jerry, as he was being released!

When Jerry finally came out he was on crutches with his legs wrapped and bandages on his head and ears. He said he had to go back to the doctor the next morning.

As it turned out, Jerry came home with me that night. On our way home, we started talking about the accident. I asked Jerry if he remembered our conversation of several months earlier in Delaware. Jerry and I had roomed together while on a visit to DuPont Paint Company to review some new paint and a tour of the plant. That evening we were talking about the three accidents he had over the previous years.

First one was while he was bow hunting and fell asleep in his tree stand, falling out of the tree. When he regained consciousness he was laying on the ground with his arrows lying all around him. He had no idea how long he was unconscious.

The second accident happened when he was working on a tractor and it slipped off the jack pinning him under it. The rescue squad had to raise the tractor to get him out; thankfully he only had several broken ribs.

Third, Jerry fell asleep while driving home in his truck with the slide in camper in the back, ran up the guide-wire of an electric pole, flipping over totaling the truck and camper. Jerry came out of it reasonably well off with only a few broken ribs and minor injuries.

As Jerry and I sat in the motel room talking about these accidents I said, "I think God is trying to get your attention and you better start listening!" Little more was said that evening concerning the accidents.

Jerry said he remembered our conversation. I told him I feared for his life as he wasn't listening to God. He didn't say much and our conversation went to his pain and the schedule for the next day. When we got home, Jerry ended up sleeping on the couch outside our bedroom and he moaned in pain most all night.

The next morning we had breakfast and Bonnie went to the Christian Book Store where she volunteered, as Jerry and I waited until it was time to leave for his doctor's appointment. As we were waiting, Jerry asked for another cup of coffee.

While going to the other side of the house and kitchen, God spoke to me, "Pray for Jerry." Being new to all this, I said to the Lord, "I can't pray for him, he's not a Christian" The Lord again said, "Pray for him". I finally conceded, okay I'll pray for him, but when I got back to the living room Jerry was asleep, I thought I was off the hook, but God said, "No, pray for him" I sat his coffee on the wood stove and waited for Jerry to wake up.

A little while later Jerry opened his eyes and I immediately told him I had to pray for him. I didn't wait for an answer as I went over to the couch and knelt in front of him, laid my hands carefully on his legs and started praying. I don't remember what I prayed but it was a short prayer.

As soon as I stopped praying, I looked up at Jerry, he looked at me and said in a very demanding voice, "What did you do to my legs?" I was elated! I knew the Lord had touched his legs. I told Jerry, "The Lord has healed you." I could tell Jerry was startled as he kept patted his legs, got up and walked around without his crutches. I didn't know what else to say to him as he didn't say much as we prepared to go see his family and for his doctor's appointment.

We stopped by to see his wife but he didn't tell her what happened. Then on the way to the doctor's appointment, the pain started coming back. As we drove home that afternoon, I asked him if he knew what happened today. He didn't look at me but said, "I know."

As I looked back on the day's events, I realized the Lord was confirming to me that the prophetic words spoken were true. I kept in contact with Jerry and his wife and a year later Jerry left his wife, quite his job with the State and went into business for himself, but was drinking heavily.

A Time to Move

Winter was almost over and spring was coming full speed ahead, when I received a phone call from Dave Hathway. Dave told me they were going to fill the Ranger position at Rocky Gap and I had two weeks to let him know if I wanted the transfer. The time had come for the fulfillment of God's word and all I had to do was say, "yes."

Over the next several days I started thinking about the transfer and what I had at Calvert Cliffs and what I would be getting myself into at Rocky Gap. As the days went by I had compiled a list of reasons why I needed to stay at Calvert Cliffs and not transfer but I was in turmoil with making a decision.

Two days before I had to give my answer to transfer I went to a prayer meeting at the Potts's home. Everyone sat down in somewhat a circle in their living room and as everyone was getting settled, I asked them to pray for me so I would know if I was to take the transfer or not.

Soon everyone was quiet and I was praying for direction when the Lord spoke to me and said, I was to go. I sat for a moment then I said to the Lord, "But I can't go, I have this list of reasons why I shouldn't go." But as I tried to bring the list of reasons to memory I couldn't. No matter how hard I tried, I couldn't bring one reason to memory. It seems when God has a plan, you can't argue with Him! I opened my eyes and said to everyone, "Did God say anything to you?" no one answered.

Then I said, "God told me I was to go." As soon as the words came out of my mouth that peace that passes all understanding came over me and without question, I knew I was to take the transfer, for the peace of the Lord was mine.

During the weeks before the transfer, I had another unusual thing happen. On different occasions three different people from our church came to me saying, "The Lord gave me this scripture for you "..." Matthew 13: 57," "Only in his home town and in his own house is a prophet without honor." How do you receive something like this, especially coming from the Methodist church? I knew God was telling me something. Was I a Prophet? What should a prophet feel like? I didn't feel like a prophet but there was something stirring inside. Was I prepared for what was ahead?

The next thing I knew I was starting my first day at Rocky Gap State Park, but it would be several weeks before Bonnie and the kids would be moving. They stayed so Robby, Gretchen and Ginger could finish their school year.

Soon we were getting settled in and we were back to our home church at Glendale Church of the Brethren. It wasn't long before I was teaching the Young Adult Sunday School Class. Over the next year, we attended several other churches but came back to Glendale.

We were chosen to attend the Holy Spirit Conference in Indiana for the Brethren and Mennonite Churches, although our pastor never taught about the Holy Spirit. We accepted the offer to go but I said I would like to share about the conference sometime during a Sunday evening service.

Shortly after the conference, Reverend Harper said he was to be out of town the next Sunday and I could do the evening service. That evening as I stood at the pulpit to start my message on the Holy Spirit Conference, there sat Reverend Harper in the back of the church. It was like someone threw a bucket of cold water on me, I knew I couldn't give the message I wanted to give. The moving of the Spirit was quenched and I'm not sure what I spoke about that evening.

During our time at Glendale, I was nominated for a vacant Deacon position. In the Church of the Brethren, a Deacon is actually an Elder. The evening of the vote I knew I wasn't going to be voted in, and as it happened I was one vote short of the nomination. This was to be, as my mother wasn't there nor were several of our close friends. It was as if the Lord was saying it is the right calling but the wrong place.

A Word for the Church

One Sunday we were at Glendale during the evening service when the Lord started speaking to me, "Prophecy!" Can you comprehend what this meant!

First, the Brethren Church never had a prophetic word spoken in the church

Second, the word the Lord was speaking to me wasn't very encouraging; it was more of a reprimand

Third, even though I knew it was the Lord, could I do it?

Finally, I put a fleece before the Lord to test the validity of the Word; to test the Spirit. I didn't want to be wrong with this word. "Lord, if you want me to give this word, have the pastor call on me to give the closing prayer."

As the service continued, I was in turmoil. I finally conceded that I would do it and to put it in simple enough words, it wasn't going to be pretty! Pastor Harper finished his message and the closing song was being sung. Next came the closing prayer. He kept looking my way as the song was finished and he began his closing remarks. He was looking right at me and I knew he was going to call on me for the closing prayer.

Within a microsecond of him speaking my name, there was a disturbance in the back of the church. It was our son, Robby, walking in with nothing on but gym shorts and tennis shoes! He walked up to me to tell me there were people at the house to see us. In a fraction of a second, the tension was broken and I knew the Lord was testing me. You may ask, How do you know?" and I would have to answer, "You just know!" From experience of walking with the Lord, you learn to hear His voice and sometimes it isn't an audible voice but a response of the Holy Spirit. I can't emphasize this enough! "You know, without Question!"

Encounter at the Park

It was Friday night and I was working the midnight to eight shift. It had been a fairly quiet evening. I just finished patrolling the campground and was headed back out to the camp office. As I approached the entrance gate to the campground a man was standing by the gate when the Lord spoke, "He's a Christian." My first reaction as I looked at this scruffy guy was,"Right!" Soon I heard his story of how they had broken down on South Mountain and knew they were going to be too late to get into the Campground when they prayed that someone would be there to let them in.

I found their campsites and let them into the campground. The next day I stopped by their campsite and we talked for a while and exchanged names and phone numbers.

As it goes so many times we have the best of intentions but never follow up on making contact. The following summer I received a phone call at home and it was John wanting to know if I could get them a couple of campsites. I told him I would check when I went on duty the next day. He said their pastor was coming up and he would like me to talk to him. The thought ran through my mind, "Sure but what is he going to tell me that I don't already know?"

That weekend they arrived and set up camp. John told me their pastor was staying at the Holiday Inn in Cumberland as he didn't camp. Later that day I stopped by their campsite to meet their pastor.

Al Meyers was a pretty big man at about six foot four and weighed about 250 - 300 lbs. We sat in their tent and talked for some time. Al was a very likable person and we connected right from the beginning. Later as we were talking Al asked me what I thought my calling was.

As I had never really thought about it much, I said I wasn't sure maybe Evangelism or something like that.

Al started speaking and as he talked, I knew there was something different about this. It was like he already knew me and I then knew the Lord was speaking through him to me. Al spoke with authority and he spoke things he couldn't have known. I knew he had my number and all I could do was listen in awe! After Al finished he told me that if this was of the Lord, it would be confirmed.

Confirmation Comes

Over the winter we started having a prayer meeting in our home. Three couples who were our close friends most always came and any number of others. It wasn't unusual for there to be as many as twenty different people there some nights.

During the first summer after moving, I met Jim Lindsey. Jim was from California and we developed a friendship. The Lindsey family was going to church with a group called, "Christian Gathering." Numerous times we attended their meetings and when they had a special guest speaker, we would go hear them.

We made plans to go hear Richard Lambert who was a Prophet from Delaware. I had heard him before and his prophetic words were right on and ministered to those he spoke to. This night wasn't any different. Before his message he had prophetic words for three or four different people and then after the message, he spoke to several others. As Richard was finishing up the evening, he walked over to our side of the meeting room and looked at me.

As Richard started speaking, I can still remember the words; as he started explaining how people are different, using himself as an example of how some people can get all excited, scream yell and jump up and down. He said he probably did all three but he said that wasn't me. Then he went on to say he saw a quality of leadership in me and the people with me shook their heads in acknowledgment of what he said.

I remembered what Al Meyers had said the summer before, now I was hearing the same thing from Richard. This was the first time I had something like this happen to me, to have a word from the Lord and then confirmation was an exciting experience but then to have the prophecy from Richard on tape as well! This would be the first of many prophetic words I would have on tape over the coming years.

Prophecy

Let me jump into my teaching mode for a moment; "Prophecy", what are we talking about? Now I know there will be those who have experienced prophecies before and then there will be those who have no idea what I am talking about, bear with me for a short discourse on prophecy.

Let's define prophecy as God speaking through someone to you or me, saved and unsaved. Yes God can do that! According to scriptures, there were prophecies to churches, towns, nations, and individuals.

Remember the scripture says God is no respecter of persons or people. Now let's go to I Corinthians 14, read and reread this whole chapter. Now let's focus on the part where it says the spirit of the prophet is subject to the prophet. In other words, anything said by a prophet is going to have a little of the prophet attached to the words of God spoken.

Let me put it like this; when I speak the Word of God, it is going to be affected by me, how I receive the Word, what I think the Word means and my relationship with God. The closer I am walking with the Lord, the clearer I will receive the Word and the least amount of my thoughts will be interjected into the prophecy, the purer the Word from God.

Now with this particular prophetic word which I transcribed on paper from the original tape, I could see exactly when God was speaking to the Prophet and when the Prophet was giving his interpretation of what the Lord had just spoken, filling in his understanding. This can be very good or in some cases not so good. This calls for discernment! In chapter 14 of 1 Corinthians, it also says to let two or at the most three prophets speak, THEN, let the others weigh carefully what has been said.

Now from my experience and for the most part, this is almost never done. If we are going to weigh something and to go a step further "Weight Carefully," what are we doing? We are looking for the accuracy of the Word as measured by the Holy Spirit. It has to come in line with the Word of God. That is what we are shooting for in prophecy, accuracy! What God is saying to me.

Then in I Corinthians 13 it says we prophesy in part because we know in part. In other words, God isn't always going to give us a total understanding of a Word from God, Why? Because we are to walk by faith, not relying on an imperfect Word. With all that said, prophecies are not bad. God can use a word to encourage us, to give us focus or direction.

Another comparison; prophecy is a tool, just one of the gifts of the Spirit. Like any tool, we have to learn how to use it properly and the only way we can do that is trial and error. Like anything else we learn from experience and the only way we can get experience is by using the tool or gift.

Scripture tells us to test the spirit; again this is my experience with the Holy Spirit and prophecy.

It is hard to explain a lifetime of experiences in a few paragraphs, some things have to be experienced for it to be real.

For example, I have had an interest in making pottery for many years. I read many different books on the subject and even made a crude kiln and tried firing some simple pieces of pottery, with total failure. It wasn't until I had some one-on-one teaching of the proper way to do certain critical steps, along with many hours of practice was I able to make a basic piece of pottery. Let me say that first piece of pottery wasn't perfect but it was an encouragement to improve my understanding and skills until I was able to make pottery worthy of selling.

Just like pottery, learning the ways of the Holy Spirit is a lifetime process. We will never be at a place where we have total understanding. It's just not going to happen! Every experience gives us a little more of the bigger picture and the more we learn and experience the more we realize we have just scratched the surface. We need to fully understand the scripture, "God's ways are not our ways." In this lifetime we will never, and I mean never, totally understand the things of God.

Scientists have studied the human body for centuries and have come up with some pretty good ideas as to how the human body functions but their best explanation as to our origin is that we evolved from pond scum? It is easier for the scholars of the world to accept the idea we evolved from pond scum rather than accept the fact we were created in the likeness of God.

I always liked the analogy, statistically speaking, "it would be easier for a tornado to hit a junkyard and create a Boeing 747 then for just one cell of bacteria to have just happened." Let your scientific mind wrap around that one, statistically speaking it is a number to the umpteenth power that we probably can't even figure the name of, too many zero's! That is the analysis of some scientist who has some idea of common sense.

A Prayer Meeting

O ur prayer meetings were always a mixture of sharing things that had happened during the preceding week; concerns, prayer needs, prayer time, question and answer sessions and most always fellowship over food! These meetings were most beneficial for building relationships and opening people up to communicating their personal needs and concerns, just like a family would do, or at least should do!

During one of our meetings, I received a phone call from my cousin who was working at a gas station in Cumberland. Rodger is my first cousin, son of my Dad's youngest brother. Rodger came to our meetings sometimes but this evening he had an unusual request. As he filled me in, he said he was pumping gas for a guy who was in Cumberland to see if the Lord was sending him here and he wanted me to talk to him. Soon I was in deep conversation with Pat Malone. He said he felt the Lord was directing him to come to Cumberland and was there to seek confirmation. We talked a little longer and he said he would call me and let me know what happened.

About six weeks went by before I heard from Pat again. He called to tell me he had already moved to the area and was living in Bel Air just west of Cumberland. We kept in contact with each other talking usually every week or two by phone. Pat became involved with the Christian Radio Station in Grantsville and the church there.

During this time many different things were happening, the pastor of our church in Southern Maryland was transferred to Center Street Methodist Church in Cumberland. We attended for a short time then started meeting in our home on Sunday until the Lord told me to step away.

Next, we attended Christian Gathering, an independent group of young believers who were meeting in different places until they purchased the old Penn Avenue School. This group was a very outgoing church but with a group of four elders who were of equal plurality in leadership, in essence, four heads on one body. The co-equality of leadership wasn't something new. This movement began sometime before on a national scale but by this time, some of the founding leaders saw some problems with the teaching and went with a head pastor and did away with the co-equality structure. Before long, internal struggles began to emerge, and as the months went by, there didn't seem to be any closure even though the national leaders gave up on the teaching.

The Staff

O ne Sunday morning as we were getting ready for church the Lord began speaking to me about the authority of God and the staff of Moses being a symbol of God's authority. I had cut a staff several years before but I didn't remember what happened to it when the Lord showed it to me in the corner of our shed. I went to the shed and it wasn't on the floor but in the loft of the same corner.

I called several friends whom I trusted to pray for me and to ask for guidance. The Lord wanted me to go and present the staff to each one of the elders and to ask if they could take the staff as a sign of God's authority as head of the church.

I entered the church that morning with the staff in hand, not one person questioned me as to why I had the staff. I went to the Elders and asked if I could speak to the church and they indicated that I could, again never questioning why I had the staff. Later during the service, I was called to the stage in front of the church where I gave a simple explanation of what the staff represented and the scriptures associated with it.

I then approached the Elders and asked them one by one if they could take the staff as the authority of God. One by one each rejected the staff until I came to the last one, Emanuel Miller. He said he could take it and I handed him the staff and said. "With this comes the authority of God." Silence filled the congregation, not a word, until the people started stirring around to leave.

Later I was told that one of the Elders secretly went and hid the staff behind the stage not thinking anyone saw him.

Soon after I was called before the Elders to give an explanation of what I did and wanted to know if I thought I was a Prophet, to which I responded, "I was just being obedient to the direction of God."

In the following weeks the church split. An interesting thing happened. I received a card in the mail from the music director thanking me for my obedience and was encouraging me to continue and be faithful to what God was doing in my life. Two weeks later her story was different as the Elders had a talk with her and many of the church members.

Several of my friends told me I was wrong to do what I did but came back to me years later and said I was right.

After leaving Christian Gathering with Emanuel, we stayed with him for about a year until one Sunday morning the Lord said it was time to leave. Not knowing where to go or just what to do, we stayed on for about six more weeks until we went to Pat Malone's church, Love's Way. Originally meeting in the Centennial Hotel west of LaVale, they started meeting in the old Mennonite Church in LaVale. Bonnie played the piano the very first service they had in this building about a year before.

For eighteen years we attended Love's Way. This was home, we had many friends there and our families grew together. When Pat's wife left, leaving him with the five children, the church family gathered around him and the children as any family would. Two years later Pat met Libby at a church in Winchester, Virginia, and her two two daughters. I spent many hours getting her house in Virginia ready to sell. Things seemed to be going well and I even helped remodel Pat's house in LaVale to accommodate the new family.

During our years at Love's Way, I experienced some great growth and one of the best Prophetic Workshops I have ever seen. Every year a Leadership Conference was held, usually, in Cincinnati, Ohio. Part of this conference was a prophetic workshop. Here you could go and a team of Prophets would pray over you, giving you a prophetic word. Several teams were praying in different parts of the room. Each team member would take turns praying and everything was recorded on a master tape and the individual received a copy of the prophetic words given. That way there was never any question as to what was said.

The first time I went to see what was going on, I had no intention of receiving a prophecy. As the room filled up there was a second room opened and part of the group started moving out. As they were leaving, the leader of the prophetic workshop took hold of my hand and said, "Come with me." I went along to the other room and they started speaking to the different people as they came into the room. Soon it was my turn and I wasn't prepared for what was about to take place.

Three different Prophets spoke or prophesied over me, the words were personal; spoken directly to me and most assuredly there were things these individuals couldn't have known on their own.

The next year at the conference Phil wanted to go to the prophetic workshop. I told him about it and said I would go with him. While waiting for his turn, a lady was being prophesied over by several Prophets. As they were speaking the Lord showed me somethings about her. I went to Mindred who was in charge and I told him what I was being shown. He said to go and present it to her when the others were finished. After speaking to her, I went back and waited with Phil. Again when the next person came up for a prophetic word the Lord showed me something for this person. Again I went to Mindred and he said to go present it to him. When I was finished I went back to my seat with Phil. Then the next person turn came up and again the Lord gave me a word for this person. With that Mindred, told me to stay up with the other Prophets as he smiled at me.

He had seen something the year before when he took me to the other room but I wasn't ready at that time. All in God's timing!

As one of the gifts of the Spirit, the church as a whole doesn't know what they are missing or have rejected.

Now with that said, you can go into many churches and they will tell you they believe in the Gifts of the Holy Spirit and yes there are those moments in which the Gifts of the Spirit are permitted to operate. I was told in one church that the morning service was for teaching. How do we tell the Holy Spirit when and where he can operate? My point is this if the Holy Spirit doesn't have the freedom to move as he pleases, the church loses! It's a matter of who's in charge!

A Moment in Time

What was to come couldn't have been explained or expected. On three different occasions, over what I think was about two or three months I had a flashback. This is the hard part, as it didn't mean anything until later. Each time I had a thought go through my mind but before it registered it was gone. It's one of those things where you just shake your head and go, "HUH! What was that?" And then you continue with what you were doing, not giving it much thought. This happened three times but as nothing registered, there was nothing to ponder.

An example in an attempt to explain; the flash of a camera, let someone flash a camera when you are in a totally dark room when you don't know it is going to be flashed, what did you see? You know there was a flash but that is just about all you know. Now there was a picture in that instant which we can print out to capture that moment in time but without the ability to print a picture in my mind there is nothing. Something was there and you know it but couldn't recognize it.

Next came the revelation. If you remember back earlier in my story, I told about the prophecy of judgment on the United States. I had been receiving a newsletter from one of the prophets concerning the prophecy and their views of what the Lord was doing in our country. In one particular newsletter, I was reading about what they were seeing happening in different parts of the country.

The newsletter was divided alphabetically; A, B, C and so on. As I was reading the different segments I came to the letter "O" (Olie), not giving it any thought when all of a sudden the lights came on! It was beyond words.

This was describing the dream of my youth!

At that moment my mind was reeling from the revelation. I was awakened to the dreams that I had totally forgotten for all these years. At the same time, I understood the three flashbacks I had were tied to the same dreams. I was overwhelmed with all the revelation. How could this be? Why now, as I was reviewing the dreams I had repeatedly as a young boy, it all came back!

The dreams were of turmoil and spiritual terror. As I can best describe it I was being chased by a ball of evil energy and my challenge of getting away from it as the landscape before me was continuously changing from moment to moment. One minute the ground was smooth and I could make headway running from this evil pursuer. Then all of a sudden large boulders would roll in my pathway impairing my progress. Next, it might smooth out again or large jutting rock formations would shoot up out of the ground and I would have to work my way over and around these obstructions. Never knowing what would come next, the ground might be smooth again or it might be like someone dumped a massive load of bowling ball size boulders in my path and I would have to jump over them or try to straddle them as they were rolling.

All this was happening as I was being pursued by whatever this evil thing was. It was never too far behind me, never catching me but I was never able to get away from it. I can't say how many times I had this dream or how long it went on but I know it was many times.

As I look back at these events and what the Lord is trying to show me I am almost afraid to put in writing what I am thinking. Although this could almost be anyone's life journey of the ups and downs, struggles and victories. In my overview of these events and more recent events I saw a pattern.

As a baby, I was told I almost died of pneumonia, then in 1966 I could have been killed in a car accident. I was thrown out of my 1964 Malibu convertible, taking the passenger door off as I was thrown over the bank. Then again in 2003 when my brother and I were in the airplane crash at Mexico Farms Airfield. My brother went through fifteen and a half hours of surgery to put his face back together and

I had 60 some stitches in my forehead, a dislocated ankle and lower spine injuries.

I was semi-conscious for two and a half days, but somewhere during this time I had an encounter with Jesus. As we talked I remember I didn't want to come back. Although I know we talked for sometime, I only remember the last thing he told me, "I want you to go back for I have more work for you to do". Looking back at this, I know the enemy of our soul wants me dead but then you have to ask; "Why me, am I that much of a threat?" But then again, any Christian is a threat to Satin!

While recently doing a word search I came across a scripture in Isaiah which tells of my life's journey. Again it always amazes me how God reveals things to us.

Isaiah 42:16
16 I will lead the blind by ways they have not known, along unfamiliar paths I will guide them; I will turn the darkness into light before them and make the rough places smooth. These are the things I will do; I will not forsake them.

God in his Great Mercy has done all of these things in my life, but see these promises are not only for me they are for everyone who is called by God!

As I am writing, it becomes more clear. It comes to light just how foolish I have been. How we must try God's patience as we walk out our journey here on Earth and again it just proves God's great love for us.

John 3: 16
16 For God so loved the world that he gave his one and only Son, that whoever believes in him shall not perish but have eternal life.

1 John 1:5
5 This is the message we have heard from him and declare to you: God is light; in him, there is no darkness at all.

Numbers

Throughout my Christian walk numbers have been a part of my life. Just like a set of directions we have to follow the numbers,"one, two, . ." and proceed to the next until we complete the task at hand.

Like the time I saw the tag number on the vehicle and I was directed to fast. See, it's not just the number, it's the witness of the Holy Spirit connected with the number. But that wasn't the beginning! Somewhere along the way, I realized there was a pattern forming, within the course of events I had to admit it was beyond mere happenstance for it was repeatable and one number was repeating itself.

When I worked at Bendix the last three digits of my clock number was "111", when we moved to Point Lookout the last three number of our phone number was "111". After I finished law enforcement training at the State Police Academy and I was issued my new badge and yes my badge number was, "111"! This number became a guidepost for many things that would happen in our lives.

While building our home we needed to get a loan to do the work. We never borrowed that much money before. We never had a credit card, so it was a big deal to borrow money. On our way to Baltimore to sign the paper for the loan, we were still a little unsettled on borrowing money.

Bonnie was driving and I was looking out the window, when I saw a license plate leaning up against a post along the road. The only part I could see above the grass was the number "888". At that moment I knew the last three digits on the odometer was "777", I asked Bonnie what the numbers were and she said, "777", now you take "777" from "888" and you have "111"! I knew this was confirmation to go ahead with the loan. It was okay.

Now you can say what you want and I know there will be those who will say, are you kidding me, a tag sticking out of the grass! Think about it. How could it be that a license plate along Interstate 70 would be at the exact point that our odometer would read "777" and how did I know at that moment the last three digits were 777? You figure it out!

We as Christians have missed so much by limiting the power and gifts of the Holy Spirit. Jesus himself said in John 14 that he sent the Holy Spirit to be our Counselor, to guide us in all truth and tell us what is yet to come. Because we don't understand or see the Holy Spirit, we hinder his workings in our lives and how he can work through us, God help us all. This should be a priority in the churches. The empowerment of the Holy Spirit was set in motion at the beginnings of the church as the Apostles spread the words of Jesus along with signs and wonders of the Holy Spirit. The world was never to be the same again as Christianity spread. Even the power of the Roman Empower couldn't stop what God had put in motion!

As long as Satin can perpetuate his lying charade within the church, the church will never fulfill its full potential until the body of Christ can come together in Unity, grow in the gifts of the Spirit and the operation of the Holy Spirit. But God has a plan and will have the victory in spite of us.

As I see it now, the church as a whole has sat in its cushy pews satisfied to let a few do all the work, never finding their place. But through adversity comes cleansing and through the fire comes purification. If I remember correctly John the Baptist said, Jesus would baptize us with the Holy Spirit and with Fire.

Look at our country during the days after 9/11. There wasn't any bickering in Washington, people were flocking to the churches in record numbers and there was a unity within our Nation.

Now another connection to the number 111, which I have no idea how it fits into God's plan or how it will end. Some years ago, while in the Florida Keys, it was brought to my attention the things happening in Yellowstone National Park . It seems the ground was rising in different areas, fissures were opening up in areas where they hadn't before and there was a great concern as to what was going on. It is well known that Yellowstone is the site of a super volcano which last erupted some 260,000 years ago according to the scientist.

Like most people, we are intrigued by Old Faithful, the beauty of the colors surrounding the hot springs and the bubbling mud pools, not fully realizing what you are standing on. Until this time I did not know the magnitude of what was happening or the potential of what could happen. To think of a crater some 30 by 50 miles in size is almost impossible to comprehend, but the recent activity brought this closer to reality. Some scientists were saying if it blew it would be a thousand times bigger then Mount St. Helen's.

I was soon researching the park on the internet, reading various writer's warnings and the possibility that the USGS (United States Geological Survey) was covering up the seriousness of such an event which has the potential of destroying a third of the United States.

To make a warning of such a massive eruption would cause mass hysteria, national unrest, and rioting. I downloaded several maps, reports, and charts to study and later printed out for future references.

The next morning I was sitting in our motor home enjoying my morning cup of coffee, reading some of the things I had printed out. I was looking over a map of Yellowstone when a Latitude lines caught my eye. It couldn't be! The line which runs down the most western boundary of Yellowstone was; Yes! "111 degrees". I will have to say this was a little disturbing. What does it mean? The answer is yet to be known, I will store this in my memory of prophetic words yet to be revealed but yet knowing it lies there in my future somehow?

See I don't have to figure it out, God has it totally in control. My input would only get in the way and hopefully, I have learned my lesson in that respect, probably not!, but I like to think so.

Sent by the Lord

Christmas 1994, like most holidays it was a hustle bustle, because of the many demands of our time and the normal Christmas schedule of friends and family gatherings, our church scheduled its Christmas dinner the week before Christmas. With our close church family, the dinner was a joyous time with too much food and the chatter of everyone getting caught up on each other's family.

During the afternoon I started talking to Dale Hipp. Dale and his family were missionaries in Haiti but because of all the unrest in Haiti their family came back to the States until the turmoil was over. Dale and I talked for some time; I didn't know Dale although they were members of our church. For the past several years they had lived in Haiti full time and made few trips back to the States.

As we talked he mentioned a future trip to Guyana, South America and through the conversation Dale said he would like me to go with them. I can't tell you the thoughts that went through my mind, the fear and uncertainty. Why would I want to go outside the United States when there is so much work to be done here?

To be nice and not wanting to further the conversation, revealing my fears and unwillingness to go. I told Dale I would like to go but I didn't have the money and figured that would be the end of the matter.

The next day our oldest daughter was home and everyone was taking a nap in the middle of the afternoon. This in itself was unusual. I was asleep in the Lazy Boy Recliner next to the door when there was a knock on the door. Still half asleep I pushed the sliding glass door open thinking it was someone I knew. To my surprise there stood a lady, I had no idea who she was?

The conversation started with me asking if I could help her. She looked around the room as everyone was beginning to awaken when she said; "Is there someone here who needs help?" The stunned curiosity had to show on my face as I answered, "No." Then she asked again, "Are you sure there isn't anyone who needs help?" Again I said, "No," who told you? She said she couldn't say. As she was turning to leave she again asked if we were sure no one needed help. At that moment the Holy Spirit spoke; "Mission Trip!" When the Holy Spirit speaks you know and without thinking I blurted out, "Unless you want to help finance a mission trip."

With that, she turned around and said, "For the gospel? I said, "Yes", she said, "Where?" I said, "South America" then she asked, "How much money do you need? I told her I didn't know as I just found out yesterday. She took a piece of paper out of her pocketbook and wrote something on it, handing it to me and said to call her when I knew how much money I needed. With that she turned around, walked to her car and drove away.

How do you wrap your head around that! Then the questions; did that really happen, who was she? Over the next few days the questions continued; was she real, was she an Angel, why me, what next?

The next Sunday, Christmas day, I found out I would need about $1,200. Monday I called the number she gave me, a lady answered the phone but it wasn't Jeanie which was the name she gave me.

I soon came to the conclusion her name wasn't Jeanie may be her middle name or nickname, as the lady answering the phone didn't recognize the name at first but then said that was her mother but she wasn't home. After a brief conversation I asked if she would have her give me a call when she got home, end of conversation!

The week went by and no phone call. Then on New Year's Day, we had friends over for dinner and the conversation was about the visitor and phone call when the phone rang.

It was Jeanie! she said she was getting concerned as she hadn't heard from me. I told her I had called on Monday and I explained to her the conversation I had with who I thought was her daughter. I then told her I would like to ask her some questions, to which she said, Let me tell you what happened."

Jeanie went on to tell me she had been standing at the kitchen sink preparing dinner when the Lord spoke to her and showed her the trailer we use to live in. The only problem was the trailer had been gone for eleven years but that was the last time she had been on Town Creek Road. Jeanie said she turned dinner over to her daughter and started for Town Creek Road. When she came to the end of the road and she asked the Lord what went wrong. The Lord then told her to turn around. As she started back down Town Creek Road the Lord told her that was the place as she went by our house and the rest of the story we already know as she came to our door.

When I told her how much money I needed she said the Lord told her to give me $500 and I made arrangements for her to send the money to our church. When I told her I had written her tag number down as she was leaving she got a little upset as she didn't want me to know who she was. Although I knew she was from the Oldtown area by the phone number, I still have no idea who she was!

Preparation Trials

Within two weeks I had all the money I needed for the trip, then came getting my passport and all the supplies I would be needing.

I soon had my passport photo take and mailed everything off to the State Department. I rather quickly received a letter back stating my birth certificate wasn't any good. It seems my parents changed my birth date so I could start school with my friend Bobby. So I had to send to Baltimore for a new birth certificate!

Weeks went by and I needed my passport number for a Visa to get into Guyana. From the time of Jim Jones and the Jonestown disaster, you needed special permission and a sponsor to visit the Amer-Indians. Soon five weeks went by and I still didn't have my passport and I needed it the next day.

The next morning I called the State Department and talked to some lady, who told me my passport was being processed,

I explained to her I needed it to get my Visa and it had been five weeks. She asked, how long? I said five weeks. With that she said she would get right back to me. Twenty minutes later she called and asked how soon I could be there. I told her it would take about an hour and a half. After a fast trip to Washington, DC, my passport was waiting for me when I walked into the building.

The next weeks went quickly; Bonnie was very concerned that our first granddaughter was going to be born at the same time as I would be leaving for Guyana. The Lord had it all taken care of as our daughter Gretchen gave birth two weeks early and I was able to be there when Chelsea was born. When God has a plan he takes care of the details!

Final details were made for us to go to New Jersey, rent a U-haul, pick up a load of medical equipment to be dropped off in Ocala, Florida before heading to Miami. The trip to Florida was pretty much uneventful; the three of us took turns driving the U-Haul and my van. Dale's brother-in-law was going to Jacksonville to stay at his brothers' while Dale and I continued on, leaving the U-Haul in Ocala where the medical equipment would be crated for shipping to Haiti. After spending the night in Ocala we left the next morning for Miami. We would stay that night in Lake Wood and Dennis who worked for World Harvest would drive us to the airport the next morning. We then met the rest of the mission team in the airport before departing.

From Miami, we flew to Barbados, Trinidad and on to Georgetown, Guyana. We arrived in Georgetown around midnight. What a shock! The terminal inside was over one hundred degrees, (no air conditioning). After gathering our trunks, we found several taxi vans to take us to Georgetown. We arrived at the Park Hotel sometime after 1:00 a.m., then find a place to store our luggage and trunks before getting to our rooms for a very short night.

A Journey in the Sun

The next morning we met in the dining room with the U.S. Ambassador to Guyana, Daniel Boone. We gave him copies of our passports and a brief outline of travel details. Breakfast was something different; the locals don't eat breakfast, so we were given a small pile of scrambled eggs about the size of a golf ball, a piece of toast with guava jam and a hot dog sausage! (A plain hot dog!) Everyone thought this was quite funny, a hot dog sausage!

Soon we were loaded up and heading to the waterfront, this was an eye-opener. The docks were nothing more than a pile of old lumber somewhat resembling a dock. Watch your step! We had to rip up a plank so we could get on board the boat. The water was so dirty you would never know you were in the Caribbean. I found out later all the mud was from the mining several hundred miles up the river.

After some time everything was loaded onto the boat and we were headed west in the Gulf of Mexico, destination, the Moruka River. This was a forty-foot work boat with a large hatch in the middle for loading cargo below deck and a pilothouse on the stern of the boat. There wasn't any shade for the team of 15 people being an open deck. Some 2x4's had been scavenged from the dock area to stretch a tarp over the hatch cover to give some relief from the sun as we traveled out in the Gulf.

We departed Georgetown about mid-morning and traveled all day in the Gulf of Mexico until about 9:30 that evening when we arrived at the mouth of the Moruka River. From here flashlights were used to signal the Amer Indians, letting them know we were ready to start the transfer of supplies and team members. This turned out to be a lengthy process. Our boat was anchored about a mile offshore and it turned out that each trip to the village took over an hour. The Amer Indians had two boats about 18 feet long and 5 feet wide, powered by an outboard motor.

I remember looking up into the night skies and being on the water with no other light to distort the brilliance of the stars. It was like a sea of stars from horizon to horizon. I remember thinking who would believe I was sitting in the Gulf of Mexico on a Saturday night watching the stars?

Being after dark, it took two natives to operate each boat, one in the front with a flashlight to guide the way and the other to operate the motor, interesting that they know just what to do and where to go as they never talked to each other the whole time.

Dale and I were with the last team members to leave the boat along with the last of the supplies, by this time it was about eleven o'clock with an hour-long trip up the Moruka River. This was an adventure beyond anything I could imagine; knowing that the Lord had sent me here and I didn't want to miss a thing.

As we entered the Moruka River, the world changed. The edges of the river were lined with the roots of the trees ten to twelve feet long which looked like giant thousand legged caterpillars. Now remembering this trip was by flashlight, the native Indian in the bow of the boat was focused on the river giving directions to the boat operator. I couldn't get enough of what was around us; giant white water lilies, vines of every imaginable species along the banks and hanging down to the water.

To make things more interesting, throw in Miniature Islands floating freely down the river, these were large clumps of vegetation which broke loose from the bank somewhere up the river.

For some reason the other team members were riding with their heads down, I guess it had something to do with not knowing when a snake was going to be hanging down instead of a vine. I was just the opposite, I was looking at everything you could see with a flashlight, one of the interesting things was the glowing eyes along the river and they were everywhere! I asked one of the Indians what they were, he said they were alligators, nice! Wall to wall alligators!

Islands in the Jungle

S oon we came to a dock along the river. Here we would be unloading the supplies and our trunks to start the quarter-mile hike to the village. Cloudland was a community center for this area. The church was central in the village. All the villages in the delta region were called Islands as during the rainy season that's what they were, Islands! Being as late as it was we didn't set up our tents so we slept in the church putting our cots between the benches.

Morning came quickly. Waking up, I glanced up at the ceiling above me to find a very large tarantula staring down at me, trying to figure if he wanted to eat me on the spot or carry me home to eat later. It's interesting the things that go through your mind in a situation like this, but it was humorous seeing a spider that big over my head first thing in the morning.

Soon we had breakfast, then the task of setting up our tents and getting organized for the day. The main focus of the mission trip was teaching for the local pastors. Throughout the day pastors and some wives arrived from the area villages. One pastor, his wife and baby traveled for five days by dugout canoe to be with us. These teaching seminars were so important to the native pastors.

Until World Harvest came into the area a few years before, there hadn't been any outside missionaries in the Delta Region for over twenty years.

Teaching seminars were held every day for the ten days we were there and in the evening church services were held for the pastors and any locals who wanted to come. While the seminars were going on during the day, other team members were assigned different tasks. Some working with the children, repairs as needed around the village and yet others were sent out to other villages for church services. We also went to the local school for some repairs and prepare some estimates for other repairs that would be needed.

Travel in the Delta Region was always by boat. One afternoon we were going to another village for evening services. When we approached a dugout canoe with six young girls all dressed in matching clothes. I was told they were coming home from school. It struck me funny as we had to stop our boat so that it would not give off a wake for their dugout canoe only had about 3 inches above the waterline. (Nautical term; "Free-board") Our wake would have swamped their dugout canoe. What struck me as funny was we stop for school buses all the time at home but here in the Delta you had to stop for dugout canoes full of students.

The Silent Voice of God

I had been so overwhelmed by the fact God was sending me to South America, I forgot one very important question, Why? It never crossed my mind that God had a particular reason for sending me. I had been so caught up in the circumstances of my visitor and preparations for the trip it didn't matter why He was sending me. Besides, I just never thought about it!

We had arrived in Cloudland late Saturday night or should I say very early Sunday morning. The local pastors began arriving on Saturday and evening services started on Sunday. Every evening service started shortly after dark, but here in Cloud-land we didn't have to depend on a gas lantern for a generator and electric lights had been installed in the Church.

The Amer- Indians are a quiet peaceful people, very friendly and respectful of others. Being the only missionaries in the area for over twenty years they were very receptive to everything presented to them. The evening services started as most service would with prayer, praise and worship. From there several team members would bring forth a message. I could see some things were being presented in a way which wasn't beneficial for these people. I am in no way against the Pentecostal ways, I have seen many pastors shout and stomp across many stages, some very good and some making a show more than making a point.

The Holy Spirit can move in any way He wants but what I was seeing and hearing wasn't the Lord. I was greatly offended by these shouting and stomping relay teams, who could outdo who?

After listening to this for the third night, the Lord started speaking to me. At first I kind of pushed it aside thinking it was just my reaction to what I didn't like, but it persisted. After some time I finally walked out of the service and went outside to pray as I kept walking around the church. The Holy Spirit can be relentless when He has a message for you to present and I wasn't being too cooperative. Finally, I told the Lord I would present the message but I had never given a warning, especially from the Lord.

After the service I talked to Dale about what the Lord wanted me to do. He was the only person I knew I could trust to give me some kind of an objective opinion. He also gave me some insight into what was happening, I was not the first!

Now I waited for an opportunity to find this person alone, as the evening went on so did the line of people. Finally, after several hours, the lines of people stopped and I was able to have a quiet moment to present what the Lord had told me. The Word was received without any response and I finally was able to leave the church for my task was completed.

No sooner had I left the church when a peace that passes all understanding came over me. I could have gone down to the corner and caught a bus home, my job was finished! But of course you don't have buses running in the middle of the jungle. Besides there are no roads and I had many days before we started our return trip.

Jungle Ministry

As I said before, travel in the Delta Region was all done by boat and to do an evening service at some of the more remote churches, we would leave two or three in the afternoon to be at the village by 6:30 or 7:00 PM. Words could never describe these three to four hour trips. The enormous water lilies and lily pads, birds of all kinds, different animals, tropical flowers and trees along the banks of the rivers. Then there was the weather!

During one of our trips a rainstorm hit and I mean it hit. It rained so hard even with a rain suit, plastic bags over our heads and a green tarp over everything we were soaked to the bone. There wasn't a dry spot to be found. Fortunately, we dried out by the time we arrived at the village for evening services.

Your Church Rocks

The first church service Dale and I held was in the village of Parakees. It's hard to tell just how big the village was because so much of the village melted into the jungle surrounding the church. The church was around 40 by 50 feet, built on stilts so the floor was about two feet off the ground. Three of the church's walls were about three feet tall and the wall behind the pulpit area went to the roof with a window on each side of the pulpit. With this configuration, the church was open on the three sides with several rows of benches.

Services started about 7:00 p.m. It was hard to believe there were almost one hundred people inside the church. Outside in the shadows you didn't know how many were watching. A gas lantern was used to light the church during the service and this was the only light in the village.

As with most churches, they started with worship. Music was usually with homemade instruments, including several very nice handmade guitars, Drums and various other instruments. Just picture one hundred people dancing in the Spirit, and with the church being on stilts, it gave the saying "Your Church Rocks" a whole new meaning.

During the service we were praying for different needs and had two lines coming up for prayer. After the lines were finished, I felt there was still someone we needed to pray for. I started looking around and waiting on the Lord to show me who it was. As I was looking around, I caught a glimpse of someone standing outside looking in one of the windows behind me.

I started talking to this person although I couldn't see them. I told the person outside that I was coming out, as I went outside and around the corner of the church, a young man about 20 years old was standing there.

I kept talking to him and soon led him to the Lord. I ask him if he would come back inside with me, but he seemed reluctant to do so. He went on to tell me the people inside probably wouldn't want him in there as He was the leader of a gang of boys who had caused a lot of trouble around the villages.

As we went inside you could tell by the expressions on some of their faces they weren't too happy to see him. I explained to the people that he had accepted the Lord and he was now their new brother in the Lord. It would now be their responsibility to teach him. I always wondered what happened to him but he was in the Lords' hands.

Another ministry trip was scheduled to the village of Santa Rosa. To make it a little more interesting, I was told Pastor Ben always had supper prepared for after the service. So my curiosity was stirred.

That evening again was something a little different. The Lord kept impressing on me to pray for marriages. I thought this was a little unusual, for these simple people to have that many marriage problems. After Dale gave the message I spoke to the congregation. Asking for anyone who wanted prayer for their marriage to come forward. To my surprise, probably half of the church came forward, about 20 to 30 couples.

Over the years I have learned never try to second guess the direction of the Holy Spirit. You will almost always end up being the one most surprised!

After the service, Pastor Ben took Dale and me to his home. A very simple house built out of boards with the traditional thatched roof. The inside was a little surprising, being decorated more like something you would expect in a more modern cabin. There was a table in the kitchen with a lamp in the middle along with several covered bowls. We sat down, asked a blessing on the food and Pastor Ben began serving. One bowl had flatbread something like a tortilla called Casaba Bread. Made from the Casaba Root. What was interesting is that the juice from the Casaba Root is poisonous. The roots are grated then put in a long tube-like basket to drain the juice, it is then dried and ground into flour.

The next bowl was a little surprising. There were some small fish about eight inches long with what looked like armor plating, like the shell of a shrimp but thicker. I later found out these were a type of Catfish and are found in the rivers of South America. They were cooked in a curry sauce. The shells were peeled, the meat picked off then rolled up in the Casaba bread along with some sauce, their version of a Fish Taco?

Night Time Adventures

Every outreach had its unique set of challenges; stopping for kids coming home from school, dodging floating miniature islands, clogged river channels and rainstorms. Traveling by boat is something most of us are not used to as a daily routine. Here it's a way of life. Another interesting part of any ministry trip, was traveling back to Cloudland, at night!

Leaving some of these remote villages after an evening service meant getting back to Cloudland sometimes one, two in the morning, or later! The Delta Region is a maze of rivers interconnecting and sometimes very narrow. Because of the floating vegetation, you could encounter a section of the river which was passable hours before, now are blocked. Most of the time it was just a matter of pushing your way through but it meant more travel time.

The most amazing thing were the water lilies which only opened at night. Sections of the rivers were lined with them. What a wonder to see! Along with all the beauty, there were the normal glowing eyes which lined the river banks, Alligators! They were everywhere and with the narrow clogged rivers meant they could be that much closer to your boat. So you always had to be on alert.

One particular night, we were in a somewhat narrow section of the river. Keeping to the center of the channel we were making pretty good time, when I had the scare of a lifetime! In a fairly open area with no overhanging trees or vines, I was all of a sudden hit in the side of my face, or should I say attacked! Only out of reaction, I grabbed the side of my face to find a frog firmly attached which I promptly flung off into the darkness. This happened so fast it took a moment or two to get my wits about me, as my encounter with the uninvited visitor was quite traumatic!

Heading Home

My jungle adventure had finally come to an end and the trip back to Georgetown and home began. Five of us had to be back after ten-day. We started in the morning after taking down camp and packing everything we didn't give away. This time we traveled in a smaller 17-foot boat with an outboard motor on it. First out the Moruka River and into the Gulf of Mexico. Staying much closer to shore then our trip out, until we came to the Pomeroon River.

The Pomeroon was a much larger river and being closer to Georgetown, the river was lined with homes and farms, piers and docks were everywhere. On the Moruka River there was almost never a dock or pier, normally the only thing you would see would be some dugout canoes pulled up on the bank. You might get a glimpse of a house up on stilts somewhere off in the jungle on higher ground.

After several hours we arrived at the town of Charity. This was a fairly large town on the river. The river was lined with warehouses and docks, people were going in all directions. Here we hired a taxi for the next part of our journey.

Things are quite different in some of these third world countries. If you wanted to dry your crop of soybeans, coffee beans, corn or whatever, you just lay a tarp out on the road to the center.

Vehicles had to either stop or go around your tarp. The road was dirt and very wide. Farms and fields of crops lined the road as far as you could see in almost any direction. What a difference from the Jungle Delta Region where we had just spent the last ten days.

After some time, we were at another river crossing. This time it was another river delta. Being close to the Gulf of Mexico, the river spread out over a very large area with numerous islands scattered throughout the river. When we arrived on the other side, the dock area was teaming with activity. While arrangements were being made for another taxi, we found a vendor who was selling bananas. We purchased a whole banana stem or "bunch" of finger bananas, about 60 to 80 bananas. Let me say that you have never eaten a banana until you have eaten a vine-ripened finger banana. By the time we arrived at the Park Hotel, all the bananas were going.

That evening we went for dinner at another Hotel. Not thinking, one of the ladies had a Taco Salad and gave me part of it. Salads are not a good idea in most third world countries as the lettuce is washed in water that our bodies cannot tolerate because of the bacteria. Let's just say we had a problem that night! In Haiti, we called it the "Haitian Happiness" because you were so happy when it was over!

A wake up call came about two-thirty in the morning for an early flight out. We loaded our trunks and luggage into a taxi for the hour-long trip back to the airport. Arriving at the airport for early check-in, we then waited for the airplane to arrive for our first leg of the journey home.

While waiting we started talking to another America who we found out was from Morgantown, WV and he knew people from Keyser, WV that we knew. What a small world!

From Georgetown we Island hopped back to Miami to find Dennis waiting for us with my van. After dropping Dennis off at his home our next stop was Jacksonville at Dale's brother-in-law to pick up Greg. The next morning we started our trip back to Maryland, taking turns driving, we drove straight thru, arriving in Flintstone late that night.

Reflection and Confirmation

Although I was glad to be home, coming home from a trip like this I will say is a letdown. For days I shared the events of the mission trip and finally put together a slide presentation of the pictures taken.

I even had phone calls from different people in the Annapolis headquarters wanting to know about the trip. Word had gotten around about how God sent me to South America. To me this was a trip of a lifetime and to be truthful, it is humbling to think God would use me for such a task.

Life was settling back into a normal routine, back to work and the busy schedule of park operations. By this time I had to wonder what a normal routine meant. I had to go back and review a prophetic word I had received several months before going to South America. The words resonated in my head of being given cans of food with no labels. "You never know what you are going to get until you open a can but it would be okay as you would be happy just opening it."

As I pondered the prophetic word and the journey I just returned from, I would have to say there wasn't a label, for I had no idea why I was going to Guyana. I still wonder why I never asked the question, Why? I was so caught up in the fact, God was sending me!

About two weeks after returning from South America the Lord awakened me early one morning. As I was waking up, the Lord spoke, "I orchestrated this whole trip for you to give that word". To say the least I was elated to think God would use me, but again it was humbling to think I might be worthy to be used. You have to ask, why did God use me. I am no one special. I am not worthy and I believe that is the point. God uses the most unusual people when and where He chooses.

Think of Paul, David, or how about Joseph being sold into slavery and used to save a nation.

Along the same lines, think about Moses; set adrift as a baby, raised in Pharaoh's house, exiled from Egypt, encounters God, goes back to confront Pharaoh, and leading God's people to the Promise Land. To start with, Moses wasn't a willing messenger but God changed him to be the servant He had planned. See it isn't always our willingness to follow God but our faithfulness to obey God's plan for our lives. He will use us in spite of our failures and faults.

Dreams

Over the years, dreams have played an important part in my life, as I have written of the dreams of my youth and after my encounter with the Lord in 1978, I have had numerous dreams which have given special focus to events and people in our lives.

Let me say a few things about dreams. You will read in the Bible of individuals who had dreams which gave them encouragement, direction or purpose. As you will find out, being a Christian doesn't give you a monopoly on dreams. The Old Testament has many individuals who had dreams which gave focus or direction as from the Lord. If you read about Pharaoh and his dreams of the seven years of abundant harvest and seven years of famine, Nebuchadnezzar's dream of the tree and Daniel's dreams and interpretation of dreams. These were direct intervention of God!

It didn't stop with the Old Testament. Paul had dreams/visions giving him direction from God. Peter had the dream of the sheet coming down with all the unclean food which the Jewish people were not to eat, telling him to eat because God was giving a new direction for the people of God, and the acceptance of the Gentiles. Let's not forget John who wrote the Book of Revelation and the dreams/visions of the Last Days and God's plan for His people.

What is the difference between a Dream and a Vision? Scriptures say, "old men will dream dreams and young men will see visions." But I like the way Daniel said it. He had visions while lying on his bed. Could it be there really isn't any difference? Dreams are usually associated with sleep when God speaks to us during those times in which we are least apt to muddle it up. Visions can happen almost anytime. Both are for the same purpose; Divine Revelation!

From over the years several dreams come to mind. A revelation from God having a purpose, but some times we don't understand it at first or we have a certain understanding and then sometime later more understanding or revelation comes. Usually when we least expect it.

Two examples stand out. I had a dream of an old house with all dark woodwork inside and it had this antiquated furnace that didn't work. A "U" shaped fitting seemed to be the problem being the wrong size and no matter how hard you tried, the fitting wouldn't fit, even though it was the right part. In this house was a Pastor friend of mine standing on the balcony looking out over the house.

At the time I had no idea what it meant only it appeared to have something to do with my friend. Several weeks later we were in church and our pastor was giving his Sunday message when out of the blue the Lord gave me an understanding of the dream.

The "U" shaped fitting was my Pastor friend, even though he was the right part, he didn't fit in the church where he was pastor.

After talking to pastor Pat about the dream and our friend, I finally called him and told him about the dream. He talked about the upcoming transfer period in the United Methodist Church. I did my part and what the person does with the Prophetic Word is up to them and the Lord.

Pastoring

A second dream I give as an example happened while I was pastoring a church in Pennsylvania. In the spring of 2002, I heard the church in Chaneysville was going to be without a pastor. I pondered the idea of offering to fill in until they found a pastor but it didn't feel right at the time. Later in August, I received a call from my Aunt asking if I would come and fill in for a while until a pastor could be found.

I had spoken there before so I accepted. After several months, they asked if I would consider pastoring full time. After praying about it, I accepted. This was a challenge for me and a great concern, for most of the church members were my family members, Aunts, Uncles, Cousins and many friends I had known most of my life.

Preparing for a message was another challenge for me. Although I had studied the Bible for years and had my ideas as to what it has to say about many subjects I had to ask myself, "Why do I believe what I believe?" Most weeks I had to dig in and study many doctrinal subjects to confirm what I was to teach. So many times we just take the easy way out and follow the traditional teaching or doctrine but what does the Bible have to say?

In October 2004, we were planning for a special three-day guest speaker and as the plans were being finalized, we received a call from our speaker saying he couldn't do the Sunday service because of a scheduling problem. Members of our church asked me if I would do the last day of special services which I agreed. I would have been doing the Sunday service anyway.

Because of the late date I wanting to get the fliers out so I entered the subject for the Sunday service as "Prophetic Vision", and although

I didn't have a special message, I figured I could give a scriptural message on visions and gave it no more thought. The services started on Friday evening and I was now focusing on the details for the Saturday services and figured I would write my message Saturday for Sunday's service.

A Two-Fold Dream

Friday night I had a dream; I was in a school dorm, it was morning and as I went from room to room, students were getting ready for the day. Some were taking showers, some were getting dressed and others were gathering their books and things. But everyone was talking about a test which was to be given. Before long I started flying down the halls into the different rooms, but it seemed strange that no one paid any attention to me flying. I then flew outside to go where the test was to be given. There was a courtyard outside with students standing around, books in hand, ready for the day but not going anywhere. I could see the building off in the distance where the test was to be given but I wasn't able to go forward. I was getting frustrated because I couldn't go and I put my foot down pushing forward trying to get some momentum but to no avail. It seemed as though something was stopping me.

With this I was awake, sitting up on the side of the bed pondering the details of the dream. As I sat there still half asleep the Lord started giving me understanding of the dream. The students inside were new or young Christians who lacked spiritual growth or understanding of the workings of the Holy Spirit, so they didn't pay any attention to me flying. The students outside in the courtyard were the more mature Christians but also lacked understanding of the Holy Spirit and were the reason I couldn't move in the Spirit or fly. This was the church!

Sunday morning came and I was concerned about how the church would react to a prophetic word from the Lord. I had taught on the subject many times but was never able to operate in the Gifts of the Spirit while pastoring at Chaneysville. As the morning service continued, I began to tell everyone of the events surrounding the dream and the details of the dream. As I was speaking the Lord started showing me more of its meaning.

In the dream, I had seen a long green grassy knoll between where I was and the place the test was going to be given and I knew it had to do with the election which was in about two weeks. I also knew President Bush would be reelected as president, and we had four years to get ready for the test which was coming. On the scene, Mr. Obama! Although at the time I didn't know who or what was coming and at the time didn't even know Barak Obama existed, I knew it was going to be a test of the believers, our faith and what was to come.

It amazes me how so many couldn't see Barak Obama for who he was, with so many questions about his past not connecting or were sealed up so no one could see them.

Let me say this; there are dreams and then there are dreams from the Lord. I can't say this plain enough, "When a Dream is from the Lord, there is no question where it came from!"

Learning to Fly in the Spirit

Concerning flying; this wasn't my first time to experience flying in dreams. Some years earlier I had a series of dreams where I was learning to fly. Starting with the very basics of just learning how to let go of my fears and let the Spirit move me. Then the next night I would pick up where I let off in my lessons of flying in the spirit. The most amazing thing was as the days went by, I would always pick up right where I had finished in the previous dream/flying lesson. This went on for weeks until I was able to leap off a cliff overlooking a large valley with no reservations or doubts, a leap of faith!

Our expectations should be to experience the moving of the Holy Spirit, but we can be our own worst enemy when it comes to operating in the Gifts of the Spirit. It is so hard to let go. We cling to the natural, our sense of what we can see, touch and feel.

Early in my Christian walk, I had two dreams where I was in a church service during praise and worship, and as we were praising the Lord I started rising off the floor only to have a person grab hold of me and put me back down. Interestingly enough it was the same person both times and he was a pastor!

PART II

←————————————————————————————————→

Doctrine, Teachings & Traditions

Over the past forty years, I have encountered many teachings of different churches and not only churches but also of individuals who had made it onto the national stage. These teachings sometimes follow church doctrine and traditions and others were bring forth new or not so new interpretations of the Bible.

So how do we know if these teachings are scriptural or not? Can we really know and where do we start? I am not here to tell you that I have all of the answers but to give you some insight and guidelines for prayer and encourage you to search these subjects objectively for yourself.

Following a message I did some years ago, I want to focus on the words of Jesus, because they should be our guide to the path of understanding and truth. The teachings of Paul, Peter or anyone else have to line up with the teachings of Jesus in order to fit into God's plan and purpose, not forgetting the counsel of the Holy Spirit.

Deceived

Matthew 24; You have probably heard or read this chapter many times.

These are Jesus' own words concerning the last days or end times and I think much credibility should be given to what He has to say on these matters. I also think it would be wise to say that everything else should line up with His words and not the other way around.

I believe it would be prudent to say His words are the final word on any subject, with no exceptions!

What about the book of Revelation?

Revelation 1: 1
The revelation of Jesus Christ, which God gave him to show his servants what must soon take place.

As the book of Revelation starts it states. "What" must soon happen, not necessarily when or in any chronological order. A lot is left to interpretation and remember this is John's interpretation of what he saw and wrote, but it's what he didn't write that should concern us. We can't have an absolute understanding of the prophecies written by John as some will not be revealed until the appointed time.

A point in fact;

Revelation 10: 4
"And when the seven thunders spoke, I was about to write; but I heard a voice from heaven say, 'Seal up what the seven thunders have said and do not write it down.'

From this, it is clear we are dealing with an incomplete prophecy. We don't know everything John saw so we can't come to a complete understanding or interpretation of the Book of Revelation.

As I explained previously, God only gives us what we need at the time. At the time of certain visions, I had an understanding. Then at a later date I was given more details or more understanding about the same vision. This is the Lord's choice.

But in Matthew 24, Jesus is talking to his disciples concerning his return and End Times.

Matthew 24: 1 – 5 NIV
:1 - Jesus left the temple and was walking away when his disciples came up to him to call his attention to its buildings.

:2 - "Do you see all these things?" He asked. "I tell you the truth, not one stone here will be left on another; every one will be thrown down."

:3 – As Jesus was sitting on the Mount of Olives, the disciples came to him privately. "Tell us", they said, "when will this happen, and what will be the sign of your coming and of the end of the age?"

:4 – Jesus answered; "Watch out that no one deceives you."

:5 - For many will come in my name, claiming, "I am the Christ, and will deceive many.". . .

First, we find Jesus leaving the temple when his disciples come along and point out its structures. With this Jesus speaks of a time when the temple will be totally destroyed. Later, on the Mount of Olives his disciples ask him three questions;

1. When will this happen, meaning the destruction of the Temple?
2. What will be the sign of your coming, and
3. What will be the sign of the end of the age?

Jesus' response is a little unusual, in light of the questions.

"Watch out that no one deceives you"

This seems to have nothing to do with the questions asked, or does it? Let's look at the questions a little closer;

First question; When will this happen? It seems this question is directed to the statement made at the temple, now nearly two thousand years later, our 20/20 hindsight kicks in play to the obvious answer.

The second question; "What will be the sign of your coming?" is referring to Jesus' return or the Second Coming.

The third question is connected to the second question but could have a much larger scope within its answer.

"What will be the sign of the End of the Age"?

Now the question is; did Jesus continue by giving his disciples an outline of "The Signs of the End of the Age"?

Depending upon which doctrine, denomination or faction you come from, it is easy to come to a predetermined conclusion; a result of how you have been taught.

Pre-Tribulation, Mid-Tribulation and Post-Tribulation, these are the main recognized views but not the only interpretations. No matter what view you believe, only one can be right!

See, there is wisdom in Jesus' answer, for He knew what was in the hearts of men. He knew the future and He knew the answers before the questions were ever presented. He had a very clear and appropriate answer;

'Watch out that no one deceives you"

Let's take a moment. What did Jesus mean when He made this statement?

First, he said, **"Watch out."** What do you do when someone says? "Watch out!"

We go on our guard or alert. We are looking for something that is going to invade or have some kind of impact on us, a pending event.

Next, it says, **"That no one"**, absolutely no one, Except; your spouse, your closest friend, your boss or your pastor? NO! it says "NO ONE", no exception!

Next, he says, **"Deceives you"**.

How do we define "Deceive"?

Definition: To knowingly give false information or half-truths in order to misguide, change a person's direction, or understanding.

Or, to unknowingly pass on false information or half-truths resulting from misinformation, misunderstanding, false teachings, doctrine or tradition.

2 Peter 2: 1 - 3

Matthew 24: 11

Deceived - Def. [Webster 1913]

"It implies some infirmity of judgment in the victim, and intention to deceive in the deluder.

But it is often used reflexively, indicating that a person's own weakness has made him the sport of others or of fortune; a victim as he deluded himself with a belief that luck would always favor him.

To mislead is to lead, guide, or direct in a wrong way, either willfully or ignorantly".

Think about it, why do we have so many Denominations, Doctrines, and Teachings?

Why are there different factions within some denominations? Misleading or wrong Interpretation of Scripture, False Doctrine!

Someone is or has been deceived, by a deceiver!

WARNING!

One of the problems we have within the church today comes from the pulpit. The church today has put a lot of responsibility on the pastor of the church. Because the pastor said it, it must be true.

Now let me clarify this statement; I am not speaking of all pastors, for many God-fearing Pastors desire to serve the Lord. Too many times the denominations have put the total responsibility of leadership and authority on the one person of the pastor.

Scriptures teach different leadership gifts to guide the church. Yes, the Pastor has the duty of taking care of the flock but he is not alone. God gave us other gifts to assist the Pastor and keep him in line with God's word.

Who remembers Jonestown, Guyana in South America? What happened there and Why?

They were deceived! They blindly followed a man and his teachings, false teachings!

Do you think they ever questioned his teaching?

This man was once a Methodist pastor. This did not happen overnight. He built a false trust with the people, probably not at first but at some point in time, he was able to manipulate and isolate them by going to Guyana.

They were deceived!

The point is this; we should be able to trust those who are in positions of authority, and the pastor is not beyond fault. He is still human.

This is the reason why God set in the church Elders with a balance of Gifts.

Ephesians 4: 11

Apostles, Prophets, Pastors, Teachers, and Evangelist.

We associate wisdom with Elders as it should rightly be, not just one man but a team of Elders.

Now don't get your tail feathers in a ruffle. This is not the case with every church, but with many. We have strayed from the original foundational building blocks of the church. Denominational organization of leadership has taken the place of the Apostles and if they are called by God as such, I have no problem with that. But they are so disconnected with the local body there can be no real input, except through the local pastor and that is sometimes limited or nonexistent.

Each body or local group of churches needs the direct input of the true Apostles and Prophets to speak life and vision into the local churches.

Within some denominations, if you don't like the teaching or direction of the leadership, you just go off and form your own little group of believers or churches.

Another example is found in 1 Corinthians 14: 29. With the gift of prophecy, he tells us two or at the most three should prophesy and the rest should "weigh carefully" what is said.

It is saying we need to question anything we don't understand or seems out of place. There is nothing wrong with asking questions, although you will find some leader who take offense if you question their authority.

We don't want to be deceived; we want to feel safe in our doctrine, teaching, and understanding.

But to tell you the truth we have all been deceived at one time or another.

Weigh Carefully

I have found within scripture a three-step process for testing a teaching or doctrine. You may ask, "Is it foolproof?" With the guidance of the Holy Spirit, I'll let you be the judge of that. I will say this; If you test anything with this process you will be less likely to be deceived.

You make your own choices!

I. Confirmation

Deuteronomy 19: 15
One witness is not enough to convict a man accused of any crime or offense he may have committed. <u>A matter</u> must be established by the <u>testimony of two or three witnesses.</u>

Matthew 18: 15, 16
If your brother sins against you go and show him his fault, just between the two of you. If he listens to you, you have won your brother over. But if he will not listen, take one or two others along, so that "<u>every matter</u> may be established by the <u>testimony of two or three witnesses.</u>"

2 Corinthians 13: 1
This will be my third visit to you. " <u>Every matter</u> must be established by the <u>testimony of two or three witnesses</u>".

1 Corinthians 14: 29
<u>Two or three prophets</u> should speak, and the others should <u>weigh carefully</u> what is said.

1 Timothy 5:19
Do not entertain an accusation against an elder unless it is brought by
<u>two or three witnesses.</u>

"Every Matter"
I believe any doctrine or teaching would fall under these guidelines.
As we know scripture can be taken out of context, proof in point;
Matthew 4:1 - 10 - Satin tempts Jesus using scriptural half-truths,
but the scriptures Satin used were taken out of context and in conflict
with others.

The context in which a scripture is used should be scrutinized.
When it comes to doctrine, it is of the utmost importance we know the
origin of the scripture. Does it conflict with other scriptures and the
two or three witnesses of scripture will confirm the truth.

There are doctrines and teachings within the church today that fall
into this trap. Are there two or three other scriptures to confirm the
issue? This calls for discernment and a careful look at what the scripture
says. We have heard the teaching and explanation so many times, we
just take it for granted

We have the responsibility for our destiny. Your pastor is not
going to stand before God on your behalf, although he will be held
accountable for what he has taught.

If a teaching or doctrine is based on one scripture. "Be Cautious,"
if there are no others for confirmation? I'm not saying it can't be, but
scripture says, "Every Matter!" And with one scripture, does it conflict
with other scriptures?

Proceed with Caution!

II. A Child's View

The next test as I will call it, may seem a little unusual but I believe it has merit when it comes to God's word.

Matthew 11: 25, 26
At that time Jesus said, "I praise you, Father, Lord of heaven and earth, <u>because you have hidden these things from the wise and learned, and revealed them to little children.</u> Yes, Father, for this was your good pleasure."

Matthew 18: 1- 3
At that time the disciples came to Jesus and asked, "Who is the greatest in the kingdom of heaven. Jesus called a little child and had him stand among them. And he said, <u>I tell you the truth unless you change and become like little children</u>, you will never enter the kingdom of heaven.

Matthew 19: 14
<u>Jesus said, "Let the little children come to me, and do not hinder them, for the kingdom of heaven belongs to such as these.</u>

Mark 10: 13 - 15
People were bringing little children to Jesus to have him touch them, but the disciples rebuked them. When Jesus saw this, he was indignant. He said to them, "Let the little children come to me, and do not hinder them, for the kingdom of God belongs to such as these. <u>I tell you the truth; anyone who will not receive the kingdom of God like a little child will never enter it.</u>

As we can see God has a special place for those who come to him as a child, and to further clarify He says a "Little Child".

Why a little child? What is so special about a little child? Think about your children, especially the little ones. The innocence and purity of those little ones, so teachable!

A little child takes everything at face value. Everything is so simple. It's as you say it is. If you tell them you are going to have blue cheese they expect to see cheese that is blue.

For example; when our Sarah was small we were joking with her and she didn't understand. We said we were just pulling her leg. A look came over her face and she said, "No you're Not!"

See, I could not have been pulling her leg. I hadn't touched her. A small child takes everything literally; they don't understand the intellect and so-called wisdom of this world.

Could it be that we should take such a view of things, especially scripture? I believe too many times we spiritualize things. Well this doesn't mean this, it's talking about something else or we just plain ignore it altogether if it doesn't fit into our doctrine. How sad!

I believe we should take scripture at face value and read it as a little child would think and understand.

One such example comes with scriptures dealing with Israel and the Church concerning certain prophecies said to be for Israel and others given to the church.

Romans 9:6
6 It is not as though God's word had failed. <u>For not all who are descended from Israel are Israel.</u>

Ephesians 2: 11 - 22
: 14 - For he himself is our peace, <u>who has made the two one</u> and has destroyed the barrier, the dividing wall of hostility,

: 15 - by abolishing in his flesh the law with its commandments and regulations. <u>His purpose was to create in himself one new man out of two, thus making peace</u>

: 16 - and <u>in this one body to reconcile both of them to God through the cross,</u> by which he put to death their hostility.

Ephesians 3: 1 - 6

: 6 - <u>This mystery is that through the gospel the Gentiles are heirs together with Israel, members together of one body</u>, and <u>sharers together in the promise in Jesus Christ.</u>

Galatians 3: 29

<u>If you belong to Christ then you are Abraham's seed, and heirs according to the promise.</u>

Galatians 4: 7

<u>So you too are no longer a slave, but a son, and since you are a son, God has made you also an heir.</u>

As I am reading this, the Church in God's eyes is one and the same as Israel, adopted, a son, Abraham's seed and sharers in the promises. So if that is the case and the Word says it, where is the problem? If you look a little closer into the issue, it's not the scriptures, it's in our being able to explain our interpretation of scripture to justify our doctrines and traditions. Scripture is not wrong, it's our interpretation of scripture!

This conflict in the interpretation of scriptures has caused more harm to non-believers. The world is watching! They do see the struggles that go on within the churches and yes they do read the Bible. Maybe only enough to see there are conflicts within the churches, which they can't understand or want anything to do with. The secular media is quick to pick up on any bit of conflict or failure within the Church and then plaster it all over the news.

In conclusion, a Child's view isn't clouded with all the traditions and doctrines of the denominations. I believe we need to take a closer look at the Bible and focus on what it says instead of trying to make it fit what we want it to say.

III. Consult the Counselor

The third point I want to make concerns the Holy Spirit, Jesus gives us explicit instructions in the book of John;

John 14: 15, 16
If you love me, you will obey what I command. And I will give you another counselor to be with you forever, the Spirit of Truth.

Here we step into what we call the age of the church. Jesus is telling us he will give us another counselor, another, meaning one as himself.

What does a counselor do? He gives advice, explains things we don't understand, gives us focus or direction when we need it.

Jesus taught by example, examples for us to follow. Now it is the responsibility of the Holy Spirit to remind us of those teachings and examples when we get off the path.

My point is this; if we put man before the Holy Spirit, we can go astray. If you go to a Christian book store, there are hundreds of commentaries and books on any subject you can imagine and most are probably good and well-meaning. Where we get into trouble is when we take what they say as gospel without seeking the Holy Spirit for discernment and understanding.

I tend to stay away from commentaries. I don't want preconceived ideas before seeking the Holy Spirit and studying the scriptures for myself, and I don't want another person's ideas clouding my search for truth if there is a possibility it is contrary to the Word of God.

Jesus commissioned the Church, empowered it with the Holy Spirit to spread the teachings of Jesus, the Word of God. He gave the Church the authority to speak on His behalf under the direction of the Holy Spirit, along with special gifts of the Holy Spirit to be used as evidence of the Church's authority.

John 14: 11 - 14
11 Believe me when I say that I am in the Father and the Father is in me, <u>or at least believe on the evidence of the works themselves.</u>

12 Very truly I tell you, whoever believes in me will do the works I have been doing, and they will do even greater things than these, because I am going to the Father.

13 And I will do whatever you ask in my name, so that the Father may be glorified in the Son.

14 You may ask me for anything in my name, and I will do it.

The gifts of the Holy Spirit are the evidence to be used to prove the authority of the church in bringing forth the message of salvation and the Kingdom of God.

Without the proof of the evidence, the church has no power to back up its authority. In any court proceedings, evidence has to be presented to prove innocence or guilt, and on behalf of the Church it is the working of the Holy Spirit which provides that evidence.

With my training as a law enforcement officer, we are taught the law is black and white and as the commissioned officer on the front line, we were to deal with the gray area of the facts of the incident. We examined the evidence pertaining to that particular incident to determine how it fits within the law, the black and white.

But as a Christian, when you are given the motivational gift of prophecy, everything is black or white. There are no gray area when it comes to God's word. It either lines up with the Word of God and confirmed by the Holy Spirit or it doesn't!

Every one of the motivational gifts will have its own slant on any and every situation affecting how we see the facts. What we are really talking about is our personalities, how we see and deal with things. It's what makes us unique and motivates us. That is God's gift to us!

Romans 12: 6 - 8
: 6 - We have different gifts, according to the grace given us.
If a man's gift is <u>prophesying</u>, let him use it in proportion to his faith.

: 7 - If it is <u>serving</u>, let him serve,
If it is <u>teaching</u>, let him teach

: 8 - If it is <u>encouraging</u>, let him encourage,
If it is <u>contributing</u> to the needs of others, let him give generously
If it is <u>leadership</u>, let him govern diligently;
If it is showing <u>mercy</u>, let him do it cheerfully.

As we can see, each gift has its own area of use. It would be difficult for a person with the gift of prophecy to operate in the gift of mercy and so forth. Our personalities are individually unique as it's a gift from God. As the scripture says, "according to the grace given us!"

Usually our personality will focus on one of the motivational gifts and in some cases one or two other motivational gifts will be apparent to a lesser degree. Again, "According to the to the grace given us!" It is these gifts which makes us unique, it is what makes you, You!

1 Corinthians 12: 1 - <u>Now about spiritual gifts</u>, brothers, <u>I do not want you to be ignorant.</u>

: 4 - There are different <u>kinds of gifts</u> but the same Spirit.
    <u>Romans 12: 6, 7, 8</u>

: 5 - There are different <u>kinds of service</u>, but the same Lord.
    <u>Ephesians 4: 11</u>
    1 Corinthians. 12: 27, 28,
    Ephesians 2: 19, 20

: 6 - There are different <u>kinds of workings</u>, but the same God <u>works all of them in all men.</u>
    <u>1 Corinthians 12: 8 - 11</u>

Paul makes it fairly clear as he states in verse one, when it comes to spiritual gifts, I want you to know what you are talking about and what you believe. It's important!

I have seen all of these gifts, services, and workings lumped together into one list and to a point that is true, but Paul separated them for a reason and it is imperative that we know why.

If we look carefully at these three verses, there is a pattern to them.

Verses: 4 and 5 speak of gifts and service but in verse 6 it says workings. The main difference comes in the last part of verse 6 where it says, "but the same God works all of them in all men." These gifts listed in

1 Corinthians 12:8 – 11 and can be manifested in or through any Christian. Whereas the gifts listed in Romans 12 and Ephesians 4 pertain to the individual as God ordained or called. We each are unique in our personalities and our ordained calling, as listed here in these verses.

Remember we have an enemy who likes nothing more than to cause confusion and if he can cause division within the church he is winning. We know whose the real deceiver!

1 John 4: 1
Dear friends, <u>do not believe every spirit but test the spirits to see whether they are from God</u> because many false prophets have gone out into the world.

1 Corinthians 1: 7
Therefore <u>you do not lack any spiritual gift</u> as you eagerly wait for our Lord Jesus Christ to be revealed.

1 Corinthians 14: 1
Follow the way of love and <u>eagerly desire spiritual gifts, especially the gift of prophecy.</u>

John 14: 26
"But the Counselor, the Holy Spirit, whom the Father will send in my name, <u>will teach you all things and will remind you of everything I have said to you.</u>"

John 16: 13
"But when he, the Spirit of Truth, comes, <u>he will guide you into all truth. He will not speak on his own; he will speak only what he hears,</u> and <u>he will tell you what is yet to come.</u>"

Jesus said, " they will live within us", here is a concept a little hard to grasp. Here we are talking about a different segment of God's plan.

Jesus is now telling us that, as a believer, a part of God is going to reside inside our spiritual being, Body, Soul, and Spirit. How does he do that?

To the world this is scary. The world and even some churches can not grasp or understand this, "ONLY by the Holy Spirit."

In the world the enemy has counterfeited the spiritual; Mediums, Spiritualist, Movies, Books, Artwork, Tattoos, even Cartoons to indoctrinate our children in an ungodly culture of lies. These are deceiving spirits! It's no wonder people stray away from the truth and the true source, the Holy Spirit.

The truth be said, the enemy has deceived the church, for many do not believe the gifts of the Spirit are for today. As the scriptures say, "they will have a type of godliness but deny the power of the Holy Spirit."

2 Timothy 3: 5

Even churches that claim to be led by the Holy Spirit lack spiritual maturity and training. God foresaw what was going to happen as we see written beforehand.

2 Peter

In the early 1900s, the emergence of the Pentecostal churches met with a lot of criticism and much misunderstanding, some not without cause! My generation grew up with them being called "Holy Rollers", and even within families, there was dissension as some stayed their distance and still do.

The church for centuries has gone through many changes, some good, some man-made but always within God's grasp.

Here was something different, a new awakening of the Holy Spirit and spiritual gifts, as spoken through the prophet Joel, "The Latter Rain", a new outpouring of the Holy Spirit.

The Holy Spirit should be the first thought in our mind and the first for our understanding, if we are to be led by the Holy Spirit or when we have a question concerning teaching, doctrine, etc....

If Jesus were here we would go to him for answers. But he gave us the Holy Spirit to be our guide and counselor, FOREVER!

When it comes down to the final synopsis, it's simple,

"Jesus said it and that settles it."

In the verses of John 14, Jesus makes it very clear that He and the Father are one and the Holy Spirit is just an extension of them, the third person of the Trinity.

So how did this deception begin?

Remember your Bible stories from Sunday school? Adam and Eve lived in the Garden of Eden and the serpent appears to Eve, twisting the words of God. The master of lies himself deceived Eve into eating from the tree of knowledge of good and evil, which God had commanded them not to eat.

From this point on, we can read many accounts of deception. Jacob steals Esau's birthright; Jonah, Joseph is sold into slavery; and the story of Daniel, Ester, Judas, Ananias, and Sapphira. These are some of the better-known accounts.

Although God used these events for His purpose, nonetheless, there was deception at the root in some fashion.

In our world today, we have to go no further than our government. Things that our nation were founded upon are slowly being torn away.

Integrity is no longer a virtue; we have to be politically correct. The moral and ethical values which our country was founded upon are being stripped away by politicians who have deceived the voter's who put them in office. Tell the people anything to get elected and then do what you want when you get into office. Why? Power and greed, age-old story!

We have no one but ourselves to blame, we have bought the lie. The church for years told you not to get involved in politics, but if godly people don't run the country, who will? The ungodly, the cheaters, the liar's, the greedy and deceivers, and now Muslims.

All you have to do is read the headlines of today or listen to the news on TV or the Internet. You can watch prophecy being fulfilled before your very eyes.

(Middle East - Ezekiel 38, 39)

The question is; has it gone too far? Have we lost God's favor and no longer coming under God's covering, can it be changed?

Are we as a nation bound for God's judgment?

Jesus warned us; Watch out that no one deceives you.

Paul said, he did not want us to be ignorant concerning spiritual gifts.

We are told to test the spirits

We are told to be led by the Holy Spirit

We are told to come as little children

We are told to become mature Christians

And we are told to eagerly desire spiritual gifts, and yes even the greater gifts.

1 Corinthians 13: 1, 14: 1

So the final question is; are we being deceived?

Are we where we should be and if not, what are we going to do about it?

It's your choice!

The Holy Spirit

I grew up in the Church of the Brethren I knew everyone and they knew me. Most families were local or relatives and most of the kids I went to school with.

I remember so many hell's fire and damnation sermons from the time I was a small toddler until I was a teenager or at least it seemed that way. Of all that time, I can't say I heard anything ever taught about the Holy Spirit. I am sure it was mentioned in some of the sermons but nothing I could remember.

Until 1978, the Holy Spirit was something I knew nothing about. Although I went to church and that was all I did, go to church! I kept a spot on a pew warm for about an hour, usually in the back of the church but any real teaching concerning the Holy Spirit never existed.

When God spoke to me, it opened up another world, one with hope, love, and purpose. I began a new adventure!

March 27, 1978, was the beginning. After my encounter with God that morning. I began reading the Bible and anything related to being a Christian. I was like a sponge, I couldn't get enough.

I was on a mission, searching for that something that would give me fulfillment and I didn't even know I was searching, until I encountered;

The Holy Spirit!

During this time our friends were visiting and the conversation turned to the Holy Spirit. I was intrigued by their experiences and I started studying the scriptures. The more I read the more I searched for answers. If this was of God, I wanted it!

I have a reason for going over these events. When Jesus spoke to the multitudes he said, "He who hungers and thirsts for righteousness will be filled".

I can't say this enough, how much do you want the things of God? How hungry and thirsty are you?

I have heard so many times, "If God wants me to have it (The Baptism of the Holy Spirit) He will give it to me" and that is true to a point.

I am speaking from experience. That is the human defense mechanism kicking in, saying, I don't want to talk about something I don't understand or I don't want to go there because it makes me uncomfortable.

Now Jesus, on the other hand, is more tangible. He was a man to believe in. There are historical records, letters and books to back up who He is, but the Holy Spirit is something else! How do you deal with someone who claims to be everywhere at the same time and lives in us? We cannot comprehend that concept. How can He be everywhere at the same time and how does He live inside us?

In the natural, these questions can't be answered, they just don't compute! But we are not talking about a worldly concept, we are talking about the Spiritual, we are talking about God's world, a realm in which we have a very limited knowledge. Jesus started opening up the door when He was preparing His disciples for his crucifixion. He told them they would be baptized with the Holy Spirit. Then He went on and breathed on them and said, "Receive the Holy Spirit." The door was opened in preparation for Pentecost and the Upper Room experience!

Can you imagine opening the door to your house and having hurricane-force winds blow into the room? This is how they explained the experience, "Like a Mighty Wind". Can you comprehend what they are telling us? They had just encountered the power of the Holy Spirit for the very first time and they are trying to explain the moving of the Holy Spirit in worldly words. It is the next thing to impossible!

The Baptism of the Holy Spirit is different for most people and each person will experience it a little differently. There aren't words to describe the awesome, life-changing power of the Holy Spirit. It has to be experienced!

Where do we start?

Some of the prophets foretold the coming of the Holy Spirit and we know some of the Kings and Prophets were spiritually empowered by the Holy Spirit.

Jesus introduced the Holy Spirit in

John 14:15 – 17
"If you love me, you will obey what I command. And I will ask the Father, and he will give you another counselor to be with you forever – the Spirit of Truth."

"The world cannot accept him, because it neither sees him nor knows him. But you know him, for he lives with you and will be in you."

For anyone who hasn't experienced the Holy Spirit or you are questioning if he is for today, you need to read these verses and let it sink in what Jesus is telling us. There is so much just in those three verses.

John 14: 26
But the Counselor, the Holy Spirit, whom the Father will send in my name, will teach you all things and will remind you of everything I have said to you.

John 15: 26
when the Counselor comes, whom I will send to you from the Father, the Spirit of Truth who goes out from the Father, he will testify about me; . . .

Here Jesus is reiterating who the Holy Spirit is, where he is coming from and what His responsibilities are.

Jesus repeats, "The Counselor", who the Father will send to confirm who Jesus is and His teachings.

John 16: 7- 11
…" Unless I go away, the Counselor will not come to you; but if I go, I will send him to you."

"When he comes, he will convict the world of guilt, in regard to sin, righteousness, and judgment; in regard to sin, because men do not believe in me; in regard to righteousness, because I am going to the Father, where you can see me no longer; and in regard to judgment, because the prince of this world now stands condemned."

John 16: 12 – 15
"I have so much more to say to you, more than you can now hear. But when he the Spirit of Truth comes, he will guide you into all truth. He will not speak on his own; he will speak only what he hears, and he will tell you what is yet to come. He will bring glory to me by taking from what is mine and making it known to you. All that belongs to the Father is mine. That is why I said the Spirit will take from what is mine and make it known to you."

Jesus repeats His relationship with the Father and how the Holy Spirit will operate within the Trinity. In these details, He outlines who the Holy Spirit is and His responsibilities to speak for Him and the Father.

Jesus was revealing to the church their New Counselor, the Holy Spirit. He felt it important enough to go into great detail to describe the function of the Holy Spirit. Even after following Jesus for three years they still had no idea what was about to transpire at Pentecost!

In the early nineteen hundreds, a reemergence of the Holy Spirit came about in Russia and then spread to Armenia. Next God started moving though individuals, then revelation was given that the Armenian people should move to America and in 1906 the Azusa Street Revival begins, the details are documented in the first chapter of a book written by Demos Shakarian, founder of Full Gospel Businessmen; "The Happiest People on Earth".

Now two thousand years later, what has happened to the church? Pentecost has lost its meaning but most sadly, the church has lost its power. As I see it, for the most part, the church is afraid to let the Holy Spirit be the Counselor. We have instituted our programs and traditionally correct teachings, not wanting to offend anyone because it might affect our attendance numbers.

Our church services are so organized; to the point, many churches have a program printed out to follow so everyone knows what is going to happen every moment of the Sunday morning service. Some denominations have printed sermon books, a sermon for each week so the pastors don't have to seek the Holy Spirit for a message to present to the congregation, as long as it sounds good, who cares?

Don't get me wrong. There are good messages, as long as they are taken from the written word and are not taken out of context, there isn't anything wrong with the message.

But! If we are to follow Jesus' teaching we should be following the guidance of the Holy Spirit.

Now the question comes up, aren't these messages inspired by the Holy Spirit?

I can't answer that question. What I can say is this; how can one pill fit the needs of thousands of people spread out over the whole world at the same time, every time? Only the Holy Spirit can do that by speaking to the individual pastors and elders of the churches.

Yes, a message written months or years before can speak to some individuals, as long as it was inspired by the Holy Spirit. But that isn't the problem. We as Christians are to seek the instruction of the Holy Spirit as He is our guidance counselor. It is the responsibility of the Holy Spirit to speak what He hears from the Father and to remind us of the teachings of Jesus. It's the "Living Word", it's a "Now" Word!

We can't take the teachings of Jesus and say I will follow this teaching but I don't understand and don't want to follow that one.

Many years ago I read a book written by Mel Tari, "Like a Mighty Wind". It tells of the Great Indonesian Revival which took place in the 1960s or early 70"s? He tells how the Holy Spirit moved through these simple people; how people walked on water, raised the dead and had great words of knowledge. This was the personal testimony of Mel Tari of what he experienced and saw during that time.

A book by Tommy Tenney tells of a church where the power of the Holy Spirit showed up in the service and the pulpit was split in half. During this same service, when people drove onto the parking lot the

Holy Spirit came upon them and they laid outside on the lawn. Some of the members of the church went to the market and the Holy Spirit ministered to people in the check out line.

These stories show how the power of the Holy Spirit when uninhibited by the fears of man can show up and change people's lives.

Comments

I will close with these final comments; the Word of God is clear, the answers are there. If there is still a question, a doubt or maybe it is something you just can't put your finger on. I would suggest you find all scriptures associated with the Holy Spirit and study them. Search for yourself, pray for guidance and let the Holy Spirit be your guide. That's his job!

Put aside denominational teaching. It should not influence your relationship with the Holy Spirit. This is the life and power of the church. How many sermons do we have to listen to about the teachings of the disciples and prophets? These are good but we need to move on to spiritual things, how to operate in the power of the Holy Spirit. It's imperative we move on in our spiritual growth, teaching the Gifts of the Spirit and the maturing of the Saints.

Hebrews 6:1 - 3
1 Therefore let us move beyond the elementary teachings about Christ and be taken forward to maturity, not laying again the foundation of repentance from acts that lead to death, and of faith in God,

2 instruction about cleansing rites, the laying on of hands, the resurrection of the dead, and eternal judgment.

3 And God permitting, we will do so.

Ephesians 4: 11 - 13
11 So Christ himself gave the apostles, the prophets, the evangelists, the pastors, and teachers,

12 to equip his people for works of service, so that the body of Christ may be built up

13 until we all reach unity in the faith and in the knowledge of the Son of God and become mature, attaining to the whole measure of the fullness of Christ.

We can only learn the ways of the Holy Spirit by having the freedom to make mistakes, trial, and error. We are dealing with a spiritual concept, one which can only be experienced. We can teach until we are blue in the face and never be able to instill the experience. We don't need another program but an environment with proven gifted leaders who can oversee the spiritual growth of the church and let me be so bold as to say this can not be done by one person, but by a team of gifted Elders operating in the gifts of their calling.

The culture of our churches is of order and that is good, but how do we learn to hear the voice of the Holy Spirit in this environment? We can teach the basics but how do you teach discernment of spirits? How do you know if you are listening to your inner desires, the still small voice of the Holy Spirit or the deceptive lies of the enemy.

Scripture tells us we are to test the spirit but how are we to test something we don't understand?

In a guise of peace and harmony we have accepted the deception. We have become the powerless church! Oh, we do have our moments, glimpses of the Glory, just enough to keep us going, but is that what we are supposed to be doing?

As long as the enemy can keep us at a simmer on the back burner we will never reach our full potential of "Walking in the Spirit".

We are told; Don't rock the boat, Don't Make Waves, Don't, Don't, Don't! We might wake up someone in the back of the church! Sadly, we have come to the place where the pastor has to do a balancing act to try and please everyone in the church, and if the pastor rocks the boat too much the Board gets rid of him.

I am a firm believer the only way the church is going to mature is through persecution, read Church history. The early Church could have been annihilated by Rome. Instead, it was through persecution, the Church grew and yes many gave their lives for their faith and yet others suffered greatly at the hands of the Romans.

Look what has happened in the past hundred years. The Pentecostals were persecuted by none other than the Church. Even in my community, the Pentecostal Churches were burned to the ground.

Let me say this; the Pentecostals didn't have it all right either, but! They had something and they were learning how to use it through trial and error also. It is so easy to get caught up in the hype of any movement and they made some mistakes just like we all do. Just in case you didn't know or remember, none of us are perfect!

Through the centuries true Christians have suffered and died at the hands of many, included the so-called church of the time.

Millions of Armenians were murdered by the Turks in the early 1900s, Armenian Christians were given a choice of dying for their faith or converting to Islam. Those Armenians died needlessly, if only they had followed the guidance of the Holy Spirit.

Millions of Jews and Christians were exterminated by Hitler, and now we are being persecuted by a liberal society and more importantly but not spoken, the Muslims. World domination is their ultimate goal and our liberal society can't see it and will never see it until it is too late! We are fighting a spiritual battle and we are not winning!

Throughout the Old Testament, we read of how God relented of judgment on Israel when they repented of their sins and turned back to Him.

The church has been given the authority to be God's messenger and the power of the Holy Spirit was given to confirm that authority. But the church has lost sight of its true commission and the power to fulfill its purpose. With so many different denominations the church is not walking in unity or maturity, the Church has been deceived!

When was the last time you went to the Guidance Counselor?

A Matter of Authority

P robably one of the more neglected subjects in the bible after the Holy Spirit is authority, as the Bible says all authority is God-given. But do we understand what it means to be under authority or to have delegated authority.

As we look at the subject of authority from the perspective of a Christian, God is the ultimate authority and as we read the Bible, God delegated authority to people throughout the Old and New Testament. This delegation of authority was not without purpose for in doing so he used people to fulfill His master plan. As we look into the history of the Bible we see a collection of people from different backgrounds that God used, Noah built an Ark, Moses was a baby raised in the house of Pharaoh, Joseph as a young boy was sold into slavery by his older brothers and Daniel was taken into slavery. As you read through the Old Testament, we find dozens of people God used. And we don't want to forget the Prophets and Kings.

The New Testament is no different as Jesus was preceded by John the Baptist and Jesus goes on to choose twelve men to be His disciples who followed him until the crucifixion, they became the first of the apostles. We can't go forward without mentioning Paul, probably one of the most unlikely of the apostles for his persecution of the church.

First and foremost we begin with Adam, when God gives him the task of naming all the animals, this is delegated authority but what are we really talking about when we say authority?

Def; Authority - (From a Biblical perspective) God is the ultimate authority, mans authority is (Delegated Authority) from God, to speak on behalf of a higher authority, to settle disputes, (Judges) to give guidance or direction, (Apostles) to give an interpretation of divine revelation, (Prophets) to give an interpretation or understanding of the written word, the Bible. (Teachers)

Over the years there has been a deception going on within the church and I have always wondered how these things were happening. Did you ever wonder how someone could look at the scriptures and focus on one or two verses and have total disregard for others which have a direct bearing on the same subject? For the past seventy years or more the church has more and more been influenced by a secular worldly system, things which would have never been accepted within the church are now being accepted as the norm.

Look at the number of Denominations we have within the Church, each claiming to have the truth. If I am reading the Bible correctly, I see "The Church", not a fragmented body of many denominations. Denominations are usually based on particular scriptures and individual interpretations of that scripture which causes division not unity. One will focus on or follow the issue of water baptism or how we do it. Another will follow the teachings of an individual or how we follow certain scriptures, others demand certain things that have to happen in a believer's life to belong to that church and don't forget the Holy Spirit.

When we look deeply into the scriptures it says we are all different and we have different gifts but for one purpose; to edify the Body of Christ. These gifts are to be used to strengthen the Body of Christ and for its spiritual growth.

We need to search for ourselves and ask the question; what direction is our church going in, are we doing our own thing or are we reaching out to others to break down the bearers that have been erected in the guise of truth.

Let's move on to an issue that is being accepted in many churches, but what does the scriptures have to say on the subject.

Lets take a look at Women in places of Authority.

For years I accepted the flow of the majority and the teachings of the major denominations. Then in the 1990s, I had a dream/vision. At first, I thought I had an answer then I had to question what I thought I believed. What do the scriptures say?

The woman in places of authority has become the norm for the past thirty years or so and the longer we go the more it is accepted.

Now let me clarify this; everyone has a ministry! And I have been ministered to by many women over the past fifty years. I have found that many times a woman is more sensitive to spiritual things than men, and I believe this is part of God's plan to balance the relationship of man and woman.

One failure within the church is that we confuse ministry with leadership, we call the pastor the minister and that is correct in function but it is everyone's purpose to be a minister of God's word. It is easier to let the pastor take over the responsibility of ministry and just sit back in our comfortable pew and not get involved or do what the scriptures tell us we are responsible for. This is not the fault of the congregation in one sense for the denominations in many cases have distorted the role of the pastor, elders, and deacons.

Over the years I have questioned numerous scriptures which the church as a whole has ignored and I have to question why?

The pastor is one of the five-fold leadership ministries listed in Ephesian 4 and I Corinthians 12; these are the elders of the Church. The church as a whole has gone so far off track there are very few churches that have elders and if they do have someone who resembles an elder they call them deacons or board members, but I never fully understood why? We have confused the whole issue of leadership and authority within the church, and don't ever acknowledge the apostle and heaven forbid you to say a person is a prophet!

The Dream

In 1996 I was on a trip to Oregon to follow up on a Solar System for Missions in the Caribbean Islands. While there we met with a member of a church lead by a lady, it didn't concern me as it wasn't the reason we were there.

From my experiences, I find it almost humorous how God sets us up for his timing and purpose. While in Oregon I had a dream. Let me explain something for those who might not understand. From the time when God spoke to me in 1978 I almost never dream unless it is from the Lord. When the Lord gives you a dream or vision you don't have to wonder where it came from. I even had Satin speak to me once and let me say, you know! Oh, you may not fully understand the content at the time for the Lord has a way of giving us understanding as we need it and to fulfill His purpose.

In the dream the Lord showed me the sheet coming down from heaven with all the unclean food on it, just as it happened with Peter in the book of Acts. Then He said, "If I was going to change the role of the woman, I would have done something similar to this."

In other words, God-given revelation.

As we know, God was making a major change from the teaching and traditions of the Jewish people. These foods were no longer unclean and God was telling Peter to eat! Now, these Jewish disciples of Jesus were to set in place the acceptance of the Gentile as new direction and new teachings of the church.

As I pondered what the Lord had shown me, I had to know what the scriptures said. This put me on a search that lasted several years.

In this search, I looked at the scriptures and what I believe the Holy Spirit was telling me. I have tried to find all scriptures on the subject not wanting to miss any that would lead me to a false or deceived thinking; only what the Lord has to say!

To maintain some kind of order, I will start with Genesis and continue throughout the Bible. I believe it is important to lay a foundation for the teachings of the New Testament Church. I will present particular scriptures found and then I will add my comments following the scripture. For the most part, the scriptures should speak for themselves. I will be using the NIV (New International Version) of the Bible as it has become a widely used version in many churches and I will let the meaning of the words speak for themselves unless there has been an obvious long term problem with a definition or understanding.

Old Testament

Genesis

Genesis 2: 18 The LORD God said, "It is not good for the man to be alone. I will make a helper suitable for him

Genesis 3: 16 To the woman he said; I will greatly increase your pains in Childbearing; with pain, you will give birth to children. Your desire will be for your husband, and he will rule over you.

From the beginning, God set in order the relationship between the man and woman and this is pretty clear the husband has the responsibility for the care of his wife. I think it is important to speak about the statement; "he will rule over you". This and the previous statement speaks of the relationship between the man and the woman. If the woman truly loves her husband, her desires will be for him. She knows he has her best interest at heart and she can trust him to take care of her. Then the question comes - who sets the rules? The man does not set the rules, God does! Oh, you are going to have a time when we as men fail to make the right decisions and our communications may have fallen short, but what do we do to correct the problem is the issue?

As for the husband; this is a God-given responsibility. The problem comes when the husband does not follow God! Entering into a marriage with a non-believer is asking for problems. With that said, there are exceptions to everything. Never put God in a box! He can make a fool out of you every time you do.

Again this calls for discernment and the leading of the Holy Spirit.

As with any scripture, it is important to read the other scriptures associated with the one listed to know if it's taken out of context.

The story from Genesis is one we know from childhood, from early Sunday school teachings we know the story of Adam and Eve, the Garden of Eden and how the serpent deceived Eve to eat from the tree of good and evil. This being the beginning of man and woman on earth as we know it today. God placed certain conditions on both the man and the woman.

Now taking the context of scripture into consideration and a little off the subject, God can use a particular scripture to speak to you about something that will only pertain to you. Even a part of a scripture can speak to you and you only. This is something only God can do and has no bearing on the meaning of a scripture or the context of that scripture. This is how the Holy Spirit works.

Judges 4 – Deborah

It is most important to start at the beginning of the book of Judges to know what the circumstances were leading up to the introduction of Deborah as a judge. Without knowing the conditions within Israel at that time could lead to possible misunderstanding.

We don't know anything about Deborah before chapter four of the book of Judges but we do know much about Israel's spiritual condition.

The story about Deborah is of interest, but first, we have to ask the question; how is it a woman is sitting as a judge in Israel? The details of this story follow a pattern of what happens when the men of God are doing evil, walking in disobedience, rebellious and not listening to God. It's important to read the complete story of what was going on in Israel at this time. Deborah was sitting as a judge because no man would do the job and it is clear that was not God's plan.

It starts by saying Israel did evil in the eyes of the Lord and for twenty years Israel had been oppressed by the Canaanites when they finally called upon the Lord for help.

Deborah summons Barak and the Lord commands him to take

the army and attack the Canaanites but he turns around and says he will not go unless Deborah goes with him. This is in direct rebellion to God's command, thus the King of the Canaanites is given into the hands of a woman and she kills him, shaming the men for their rebellion.

The Book of Esther

Ester is another one of those books where God has a plan and we see how God uses Esther to save the people of Israel. We find that Esther was a young Jewish girl of great beauty who was chosen by the king to be his wife after his first wife refused to obey him and was exiled because of her rebellion. Esther then became queen of this pagan nation.

As the story goes the Jewish people were in great peril of being annihilated, only after Esther appeared before the king revealing that she also was a Jew and Haman was about to destroy all of the Jewish people. It is important to understand that Esther had no authority within the country and it was in peril of her life just to appear before the king without first being summoned. Disobedience to her husband could mean her death. Through her craftiness, she throws a banquet where she reveals Haman's plot and saves the Jewish people.

Isaiah, God's Prophet

It would do well to read all of chapter 3, it will give you an idea of the conditions in Israel, of the rebellion and sin.

Isaiah 3: 1 - See now, the Lord, the LORD Almighty, is about to take from Jerusalem and Judah both supply and support: all supplies of food and all supplies of water,

2 the hero and the warrior, the judge and the prophet, the diviner and the elder,

3 the captain of fifty and the man of rank, the counselor, skilled craftsman, and clever enchanter.

4 "I will make mere youths their officials; children will rule over them."

5 People will oppress each other— man against man, neighbor against neighbor. The young will rise up against the old, the nobody against the honored.

6 A man will seize one of his brothers in his father's house, and say, "You have a cloak, you be our leader; take charge of this heap of ruins!"

7 But in that day he will cry out, "I have no remedy. I have no food or clothing in my house; do not make me the leader of the people."

8 Jerusalem staggers, Judah is falling; their words and deeds are against the LORD, defying his glorious presence.

9 The look on their faces testifies against them; they parade their sin like Sodom; they do not hide it. Woe to them! They have brought disaster upon themselves.

10 Tell the righteous it will be well with them, for they will enjoy the fruit of their deeds.

11 Woe to the wicked! Disaster is upon them! They will be paid back for what their hands have done.

12 Youths oppress my people, women rule over them. My people, your guides lead you astray; they turn you from the path.

13 The LORD takes his place in court; he rises to judge the people.

14 The LORD enters into judgment against the elders and leaders of his people: "It is you who have ruined my vineyard; the plunder from the poor is in your houses.

15 What do you mean by crushing my people and grinding the faces of the poor?" declares the Lord, the LORD Almighty.

16 The LORD says, "The women of Zion are haughty, walking along with outstretched necks, flirting with their eyes, strutting along with swaying hips, with ornaments jingling on their ankles.

Isaiah 3: 12 – Youths oppress my people, <u>women rule over them. O, my people, your guides lead you astray; they turn you from the path.</u>

I never saw these scriptures until sometime after I started writing, but I think they speak volumes about the conditions within Israel and what God's plan and purpose were for his people.

First, they speak of the righteous and the wicked and how they will receive the rewards of their fruits. But then God says the wicked will be paid back for their evil deeds.

In verse 12 we are told a little more of what is going on in the nation; "Youths oppress my people." In other words, the young people were forcing them against their will. These youths are obviously not operating within God's authority. Then it says; "Women rule over them, O my people, your guides lead you astray; they turn you from the path".

This is God's word and I don't think it can get any plainer. It is obvious things are going against God's plan and the nation is suffering as these women are leading the nation astray.

New Testament
Foundation of the Church

1 Corinthians 14: 33 – 40

33 For God is not a God of disorder but of peace—as in all the congregations of the Lord's people.

34 Women should remain silent in the churches. They are not allowed to speak but must be in submission, as the law says.

35 If they want to inquire about something, they should ask their own husbands at home; for it is disgraceful for a woman to speak in the church.

36 Or did the word of God originate with you? Or are you the only people it has reached?

37 If anyone thinks they are a prophet or otherwise gifted by the Spirit, let them acknowledge that what I am writing to you is the Lord's command.

38 But if anyone ignores this, they will themselves be ignored.

39 Therefore, my brothers and sisters, be eager to prophesy and do not forbid speaking in tongues.

40 But everything should be done in a fitting and orderly way.

Now to further our quest, it is the general consensus of today's church that men and women of the congregation were separated and did not sit together. This would make it difficult for a woman to ask questions of her husband without disrupting the whole body of believers.

I am not a scholar of early church history or the traditions of the Jewish peoples at that time. At the time in which Paul wrote these letters to the different churches, they were meeting in the homes of individual believer's or some structure large enough to hold a gathering. I think that would make it most difficult for any great separation of anybody.   Whispering or talking between husband and wife, or for that matter, anyone, is most disruptive in any setting. This is especially so in church when the Pastor or Elder is speaking to the whole congregation.

A point of interest; The church which I pastored for six years was built in 1860 as an Methodist Episcopal church. Originally it had two front doors, one for the men and one for the women, thus separation of men and women. This was changed in 1913 to a single entrance, when a vestibule was added with a steeple and bell.

1 Corinthians 14: 36, brings up an important point. It appears some were challenging Paul on his teachings, as he asked. "Did the word of God originate with you?" "Or are you the only people it has reached?"

Paul was in a unique position, God had called him to go to the Gentiles and proclaim God's word to them. In doing so he was writing the guidelines for the church to follow and if you remember Paul even had to correct Peter on certain issues of following the law.

But in verse 37 he further states that if you are hearing from the Holy Spirit you will acknowledge that these are the Lord's commands but if you don't then you should be ignored. These are pretty strong words as Paul was being challenged in his Authority.

I have added these next scriptures to make a point of Paul's authority and responsibilities to present God's Word. Paul was hearing the Holy Spirit, not the voice of man. God was giving him directions of how He wanted His church set up.

I Corinthians 2: 10 -16

6 We do, however, speak a message of wisdom among the mature, but not the wisdom of this age or of the rulers of this age, who are coming to nothing.

7 No, we declare God's wisdom, a mystery that has been hidden and that God destined for our glory before time began.

8 None of the rulers of this age understood it, for if they had, they would not have crucified the Lord of glory.

9 However, as it is written: "What no eye has seen, what no ear has heard, and what no human mind has conceived" — the things God has prepared for those who love him—

10 these are the things God has revealed to us by his Spirit. The Spirit searches all things, even the deep things of God.

11 For who knows a person's thoughts except for their own spirit within them? In the same way, no one knows the thoughts of God except the Spirit of God.

12 What we have received is not the spirit of the world, but the Spirit who is from God, so that we may understand what God has freely given us.

13 This is what we speak, not in words taught us by human wisdom but in words taught by the Spirit, explaining spiritual realities with Spirit-taught words.

14 The person without the Spirit does not accept the things that come from the Spirit of God but considers them foolishness, and cannot understand them because they are discerned only through the Spirit.

15 The person with the Spirit makes judgments about all things, but such a person is not subject to merely human judgments,

16 for, "Who has known the mind of the Lord so as to instruct him?" But we have the mind of Christ.

One question which might come up while reading these verses is who is the "We?" God empowered Jesus' disciples to be the first apostles to the church. They were the first to receive the Holy Spirit and were given the authority to set up the church. And we know Paul was called as an apostle to the Gentiles, thus the "WE." Verses 9 and 10 tells us what the Holy Spirit is revealing to them.

Galatians 3: 28

<u>**28** There is neither Jew nor Gentile, neither slave nor free, **nor is there male and female, for you are all one in Christ Jesus.**</u>

As most anyone who has studied these scriptures this particular one has been brought up as to say there is no difference between man and woman. If you read just this verse that is what it implies, but we are talking about Authority.

Let us look at this scripture and the context in which it is written; Galatians 3 is referring to being justified by faith vs works of the law, read the whole chapter. It is pretty well summed up in verses 23 – 29, Let's look.

23 Before the coming of this faith, we were held in custody under the law, locked up until the faith that was to come would be revealed.

24 <u>**So the law was our guardian until Christ came that we might be justified by faith.**</u>

25 Now that this faith has come, we are no longer under a guardian.

26 <u>So in Christ Jesus, you are all children of God through faith,</u>

27 <u>for all of you who were baptized into Christ have clothed yourselves with Christ.</u>

28 There is neither Jew nor Gentile, neither slave nor free, nor is there male and female, for you are all one in Christ Jesus.

29 <u>If you belong to Christ, then you are Abraham's seed, and heirs according to the promise.</u>

As we can read in verse 29 this whole chapter is referring to being heirs of Abraham by faith in Jesus. There is nothing here that gives reference to authority. If that were so, according to just this chapter and verse, everyone who had faith in Jesus would be in a position of authority.

Now that being said; Everyone as a Christian has authority over Satan but in the Church, we have to look at all the scriptures which give us our guidelines for those which God has called as Leaders.

Ephesians 5: 22 - 24, 25, 33

21 Submit to one another out of reverence for Christ.

22 Wives, submit yourselves to your own husbands as you do to the Lord.

23 For the husband is the head of the wife as Christ is the head of the church, his body, of which he is the Savior.

24 Now as the church submits to Christ, so also wives should submit to their husbands in everything.

25 Husbands, love your wives, just as Christ loved the church and gave himself up for her

26 to make her holy, cleansing her by the washing with water through the word,

27 and to present her to himself as a radiant church, without stain or wrinkle or any other blemish, but holy and blameless.

28 In this same way, husbands ought to love their wives as their own bodies. He who loves his wife loves himself.

29 After all, no one ever hated their own body, but they feed and care for their body, just as Christ does the church—

30 for we are members of his body.

31 "For this reason, a man will leave his father and mother and be united to his wife, and the two will become one flesh."

32 This is a profound mystery—but I am talking about Christ and the church.

33 However, each one of you also must love his wife as he loves himself, and the wife must respect her husband.

1 Timothy 2: 9 - 15

1 I urge, then, first of all, that petitions, prayers, intercession, and thanksgiving be made for all people—

2 for kings and all those in authority, that we may live peaceful and quiet lives in all godliness and holiness.

3 This is good, and pleases God our Savior,

4 who wants all people to be saved and to come to a knowledge of the truth.

5 For there is one God and one mediator between God and mankind, the man Christ Jesus,

6 who gave himself as a ransom for all people. This has now been witnessed to at the proper time.

7 And for this purpose I was appointed a herald and an apostle—I am telling the truth, I am not lying—and a true and faithful teacher of the Gentiles.

8 Therefore I want the men everywhere to pray, lifting up holy hands without anger or disputing.

9 I also want the women to dress modestly, with decency and propriety, adorning themselves, not with elaborate hairstyles or gold or pearls or expensive clothes,

10 but with good deeds, appropriate for women who profess to worship God.

11 A woman should learn in quietness and full submission.

12 I do not permit a woman to teach or to assume authority over a man; she must be quiet.

13 For Adam was formed first, then Eve.

14 And Adam was not the one deceived; it was the woman who was deceived and became a sinner.

15 But women will be saved through childbearing—if they continue in faith, love, and holiness with propriety.

1 Timothy 3

1 Here is a trustworthy saying: Whoever aspires to be an overseer desires a noble task.

2 Now the overseer is to be above reproach, faithful to his wife, temperate, self-controlled, respectable, hospitable, able to teach,

3 not given to drunkenness, not violent but gentle, not quarrelsome, not a lover of money.

4 He must manage his own family well and see that his children obey him, and he must do so in a manner worthy of full respect.

5 (If anyone does not know how to manage his own family, how can he take care of God's church?)

6 He must not be a recent convert, or he may become conceited and fall under the same judgment as the devil.

7 He must also have a good reputation with outsiders, so that he will not fall into disgrace and into the devil's trap.

8 In the same way, deacons are to be worthy of respect, sincere, not indulging in much wine, and not pursuing dishonest gain.

9 They must keep hold of the deep truths of the faith with a clear conscience.

10 They must first be tested; and then if there is nothing against them, let them serve as deacons.

11 In the same way, the women are to be worthy of respect, not malicious talkers but temperate and trustworthy in everything.

12 A deacon must be faithful to his wife and must manage his children and his household well.

13 Those who have served well gain an excellent standing and great assurance in their faith in Christ Jesus.

14 Although I hope to come to you soon, **I am writing you these instructions so that,**

15 if I am delayed, you will know how people ought to conduct themselves in God's household, which is the church of the living God, the pillar and foundation of the truth.

16 Beyond all question, the mystery from which true godliness springs is great: He appeared in the flesh, was vindicated by the Spirit, was seen by angels, was preached among the nations, was believed on in the world, was taken up in glory.

I Peter 3: 1 – 7

1 Wives, in the same way, submit yourselves to your own husbands so that, if any of them do not believe the word, they may be won over without words by the behavior of their wives,

2 when they see the purity and reverence of your lives.

3 Your beauty should not come from outward adornment, such as elaborate hairstyles and the wearing of gold jewelry or fine clothes.

4 Rather, it should be that of your inner self, the unfading beauty of a gentle and quiet spirit, which is of great worth in God's sight.

5 For this is the way the holy women of the past who put their hope in God used to adorn themselves. They submitted themselves to their own husbands,

6 like Sarah, who obeyed Abraham and called him her lord. You are her daughters if you do what is right and do not give way to fear.

7 Husbands, in the same way, be considerate as you live with your wives and treat them with respect as the weaker partner and as heirs with you of the gracious gift of life, so that nothing will hinder your prayers.

I am profoundly confused as to how we can ignore and disregard these scriptures. Yet go into minute detail of other scriptures to prove a point on a particular teaching we hold dear to our hearts.

I am sure there are other scriptures on the subject of the role of both men and women but I have covered the majority of them. For years these scriptures were the guidelines which the church followed but for some reason, the church as a whole decided these scriptures were not credible anymore, Why?

How do you say it gently and politely?

"The church has been Deceived!"

We know Paul had a problem as he wrote to the church in Corinth. Paul puts it quite plainly, they were out of order to question his authority. Now we don't know the circumstances around these verses but he is telling them they should be quiet in church and ask questions at home. I don't think it was meant for the women to be totally silent. But in some circumstances they were stepping out of order, interfering with the flow of the Spirit, in disregard of God's delegated authority.

We know there are differences in the makeup of men and women and I don't say this in any way as disrespect or to put either down. The man is a one-task person, focused on one thing at a time, whereas a woman is more of a multitask-er and if the man isn't moving as quickly as the woman thinks he should, he will hear about it! This could have been the issue within the churches Paul was writing to, as it has been an ongoing thing between men and women for ages, starting with Adam and Eve. Think about it, Eve was the one the serpent approached, not Adam. It appears Eve could have been in the vicinity of the tree without Adam when this conversation took place? What was she doing there?

In furthering this discussion, it plainly says the wife is to submit to her husband. Now if my wife is to be submitted to me, then how is it I should have to submit to another man's wife if they were to be put in a place of authority.

Let's go a step further and say my wife is the pastor of a church, who submits to who? At home, the wife is submitted to her husband but in the church, he is submitted to her? That goes against all of the teachings of the Bible.

This did not originate with me. It is in plain words right in our Bibles.

Now I know there are going to be those who will bring up the question of the woman prophetess. We have them in both the Old and New Testament or it would seem. Deborah is listed as a prophet in Judges 4 and I have no problem with that, but we know the story of how she got to that place. This was not God's plan but because of rebellion. Simply enough the men would not assume the responsibility!

Now in the New Testament in the Book of Acts chapter 21, verse 9, we find the four daughters of Philip the evangelist whom it says prophesied. Now in some translations they are called prophetess, which is correct to a certain point, for they prophesied but that by no means gives them the authority of the office of a prophet.

In the book of Joel, he prophecies that in the latter-day your sons and daughters would prophesy and we know one of the gifts of the Spirit is prophecy but it does not place every person who prophecies in a position of authority.

Joel 2: 28, 29

28 "And afterward, I will pour out my Spirit on all people. Your sons and daughters will prophesy, your old men will dream dreams, your young men will see visions.

29 Even on my servants, both men and women, I will pour out my Spirit in those days.

Let's go a step further, what or who is a prophet?

One who has been called of God (delegated authority) to act as a spokesperson for God, one who hears the Holy Spirit and speaks what he hears.

As a matter of Authority;

Ephesians 2: 20 - built on the foundation of the apostles and prophets, with Christ Jesus himself as the chief cornerstone.

1 Corinthians 12: 28 - And God has placed in the church first of all apostles, second prophets, third teachers, then miracles, then gifts of healing, of helping, of guidance, and of different kinds of tongues.

Here is a structure of authority built on Christ Jesus as the main cornerstone. First comes the apostle, second the prophet and third the teachers. Then it lists all of the other gifts together on the same level of authority within the structure of the church.

Answer this question; Why is so much written about order in the church, if we are going to ignore it? Yet, on other issues of interest, one verse will be dissected and every letter of a word is scrutinized and cross-examined to emphasize a point as we want it to be seen.

Remember the witness of two or three!

Looking back on the church over the past hundred years, there has been a lot of external influences. Many new innovations brought about the ability to travel, not only by train but cars and airplanes. Communication through the telephone, radio, and television made the world much smaller. Now we also have to add the internet and social media.

World War 1 was in more of a transitional period of modernization and was fought mainly in Europe and the Middle East.

But then came World War 2 which spanned the whole world: Europe, Africa, Japan, China, Russia, England, the Atlantic Ocean, and the South Pacific Islands. This took millions of men out of the workforce to fight a war, leaving the women at home to take care of the family and forced many into the workplace to supply the war effort.

Now for the women with this new found freedom came a new sense of worth, as they were free of the home and the ability to do things they wouldn't have before, but for the war. Then when the war was over, many didn't want to give up these freedoms or the jobs, causing instability within many homes. This indirectly affected the church and its authority.

So where do we go with this? Is it something that needs to be addressed or are we destined to repeat history?

According to the Bible, I believe there is need for correction. Look at the examples set for us in the nation of Israel. Rebellion and sin corrupted the nation thus bring judgment. Are we headed for the same destiny? If we don't change, we will hit it head-on, not seeing until its too late!

The matter of authority is clearly addressed in the writings of Paul and Peter as they wrote to the different churches giving them direction as to how God wanted the church to operate, and it is clear their authority was being challenged. So who are we to go against God's plan?

According to God's word the women do not have any place of authority over men in the Church, this is not my words, it's God's Word!

I challenge you to read the scriptures and seek the guidance of the Holy Spirit.

The Rapture and The Second Coming

The same or different?

When it comes to the subject of the Rapture, some will be quick to tell you the word is not in the Bible, and that is true. But the word rapture pertains to a particular event, which deals with what will happen to the church. The real question is when will this happen?

Where do we start? Many within the church will call this the rapture of the church and then quickly quote from;

1 Thessalonians 4: 15 - 17

15 According to the Lord's word, we tell you that we who are still alive, who are left until the coming of the Lord, will certainly not precede those who have fallen asleep.

16 For the Lord himself will come down from heaven, with a loud command, with the voice of the archangel and with the trumpet call of God, and the dead in Christ will rise first.

17 After that, we who are still alive and are left will be caught up together with them in the clouds to meet the Lord in the air. And so we will be with the Lord forever.

The term Rapture is used here to put emphasis the words of verse 17. Here it says, "we who are left will be caught up together to meet the Lord in the air" and as stated by some, "The catching away of the church".

For most of the churches, a pre-tribulation rapture is the most preferred teaching, which is described as an event which occurs at the beginning of the seven-year period. This is tied into verse 17, but it is important to connect all of the dots. Verse 14 is forgotten as it says the Lord is bringing all of the dead in Christ with him. Then we are raptured up to meet them in the air, to return to heaven for the seven-year period until the Second Coming. Which occurs at the end of the seven years.

But is that the way this really happens? Another great debate! Pre-Tribulation, Mid-Tribulation or Post-Tribulation. You can hear convicting arguments from all three camps, but where does the truth lie?

Here we are referencing the Seven years of Tribulation and you can read about it in the Book of Daniel. The Book of Revelation, Matthew 24, Mark 13 and Luke 21. Also known as the Great Tribulation and the Wrath of God. But then scripture tells us we will not suffer the wrath of God. So we must be raptured before the Great Tribulation, Right? Or are we?

I know many will wonder why I am writing this. For we know what the denominations have to say about it, which varies according to what denomination or church you belong to. Of all the different teachings, and there are many, we will have to conclude there is only one correct answer. Everything else is deception either knowingly or unknowingly!

My purpose is to look at the scriptures and let the scriptures paint a picture for us. And maybe, just maybe, we can come to some kind of an understanding as to what God's true plan is for His people.

Jesus' Words

To start with, I will refer to Matthew 24 numerous times during this writing. In a previous chapter, I stated that I believe all other scriptures or teachings need to line up with what Jesus had to say to His disciples. For I believe this is the most comprehensive look at the End Times or Last Days as a timeline. The book of Revelation also gives us details of certain events, but as I stated before, it is not a complete prophecy. John was told to seal up parts of it as to what the Seven Thunders had to say.

Revelation 10:3 - and he gave a loud shout like the roar of a lion. When he shouted, the voices of the seven thunders spoke.

4 And when the seven thunders spoke, I was about to write; but I heard a voice from heaven say, "Seal up what the seven thunders have said and do not write it down."

With that being said, I believe the events of the Book of Revelation need to and do fit into the narrative of Matthew 24. And don't forget the scriptures in Daniel. Oh! And by the way, part of Daniel's prophecies are sealed up too. Until some future date!

Daniel 12: 4 - But you, Daniel, roll up and seal the words of the scroll until the time of the end. Many will go here and there to increase knowledge.

Then again in verse 8, we are told Daniel asked the question a second time.

<u>Daniel 12: 8 – 13</u>

8 <u>I heard, but I did not understand. So I asked, My lord, what will the outcome of all this be?</u>

9 He replied, <u>Go your way, Daniel, because the words are rolled up and sealed until the time of the end.</u>

10 <u>Many will be purified, made spotless and refined</u>, but the wicked will continue to be wicked. None of the wicked will understand,<u> but those who are wise will understand.</u>

11 From the time that the daily sacrifice is abolished and the abomination that causes desolation is set up, there will be 1,290 days.

12 Blessed is the one who waits for and reaches the end of the 1,335 days.

13 As for you, go your way till the end. You will rest, and then at the end of the days you will rise to receive your allotted inheritance.

In verse 9 he is told again the words are rolled up and sealed until the time of the end.

So here we have the two main narratives concerning details of the Last Days or End of the Age and both have quantitative parts sealed up until God's appointed time.

To put this in perspective lets compare it to putting a puzzle together, you sort all of the pieces and start putting it together. When you get down toward the finish you see pieces are missing, you don't have a complete picture, it's not finished. You have an idea what the picture looks like but it isn't complete, you are missing explicit details of what the finished picture looks like.

As I read these scriptures, any attempt at saying I have all the answers is wishful thinking.

From the information we do have, let's see where it will take us?

Matthew 24. **4** Jesus answered: "Watch out that no one deceives you."

5 For many will come in my name, claiming, 'I am the Messiah,' and will deceive many.

6 You will hear of wars and rumors of wars but see to it that you are not alarmed. Such things must happen, but the end is still to come.

7 Nation will rise against nation, and kingdom against kingdom. There will be famines and earthquakes in various places.

8 All these are the beginning of birth pains.

As we have read in verse 4, Jesus warned, "Watch out that no one deceives you", but in verse 5, He goes on to say, "Many will be deceived".   To me this is a disturbing statement, how do you define, Many? This is not a few or some, it says many! When you look at a crowd and say many of them will be deceived, you are saying that a very large percentage of them are included.

Lets crunch some numbers:

"A Few" - 10% - 20%,
"Some" - 30% - 40%,
"Many" - 50% - 60%,
"Most" - 70% - 90%.

Now these numbers are not etched in stone but they do give you some idea of how many people Jesus was talking about.

Natural devastation is nothing new but in recent years, the intensity and frequency are most noteworthy. Even as I write, the news on television is filled with earthquakes, floods, hurricanes, tornadoes and heat waves, as it seems one right after another.

Next, we enter a period of time that goes against anything we want to experience or for that matter even think about.

Persecution isn't something we want to hear or even believe God would permit us to suffer. We in the United States have led a very blessed and protected life. We have lost sight of history and the persecution of Christians around the world. We don't want to think that something like that could possibly happen to us here. God would never permit that, or would He?

Think about this; from the conception of the church, there has been persecution of Christians somewhere in the world. Many have died in some of the most hideous of ways, impaled on poles, fed to the lions, burned at the stake, be-headed and mutilated. These things have already happened to Christians around the world and you think you are better as to not suffer. Get your head out of the sand and think again!

Matthew 24

9 "Then you will be handed over to be persecuted and put to death, and you will be hated by all nations because of me.

10 At that time many will turn away from the faith and will betray and hate each other,

11 and many false prophets will appear and deceive many people.

12 Because of the increase of wickedness, the love of most will grow cold,

13 but the one who stands firm to the end will be saved.

Jesus makes it pretty clear that deception is going to be a big problem along with wars, famines, and earthquakes, all are just the beginnings of the End Times.

Again in verse: 9, "Then you will be handed over to be persecuted and put to death, and you will be hated by all nations because of me."

Take a step back and look at these verses;

:6 - . . . . Such things must happen, but the end is still to come.

:8 - All these are the beginning of birth pains.

Here a question comes up - who is going to hand us over? I would think it is going to be someone we know and maybe have put some trust in, as my thoughts go to the secular church and verse 10 confirms that thought.

10 <u>At that time many will turn away from the faith and will betray and hate each other.</u>

It says many will turn away from the faith, these are Christians who will betray you and hate you because of Jesus. The saddest thing is in verse 12 for it says, "the love of **Most** will grow cold." This is a very sobering thought! Look around your churches. To think some of these people could be the ones to deny Christ when the going gets tough, why is that?

They have been Deceived!

False doctrines, false teachings, false prophets and teachers. I am not here to scare you but the Word of God says it is going to happen and I know what you are thinking; that won't be our church.

Why do you think the majority of churches go with a Pre-Tribulation Rapture? They can't deal with the possibilities that Christians would have to go through any part of the Great Tribulation. What would happen to church numbers when you start preaching judgment and suffering for Christ after being indoctrinated with, "I won't be here"

Look at 2 Timothy 3:5. It says, " having a form of godliness but denying its power. Have nothing to do with such people."

We are talking about professing Christians who have denied the Holy Spirit for we know this is the source of our power. These are people who have been deceived and are deceiving others. Again I cannot emphasize enough our need to pursue the things of the Holy Spirit. God is Faithful!

The church today has set itself up for destruction by denying not only the Holy Spirit but has also rejected the Apostles and Prophets. Without God called and ordained Apostles and Prophets we leave ourselves open to the wiles of the False Prophets for you have no idea how a True Prophet operates within the church.

Some denominational doctrine and teaching are based on the premise that the Apostles and Prophets have no place in the church today, no longer needed as we had the original Apostles and Prophets so they are not needed today.

With this kind of teaching, we have a problem if we read

1 Corinthians 1: 7

"Therefore you do not lack any spiritual gift as you eagerly wait for our Lord Jesus Christ to be revealed."

Pretty simple, for it says we have all the Spiritual Gifts available until Christ returns. Or what about Ephesians 4: 11 – 15, now read this carefully for it gives many reasons why we need all of the Gifts operating within the church. Apostles, Prophets, Evangelist, Pastors and Teachers, they are Christ ordained for the Unity and Maturity of the Body of Christ, the church!

Ephesians 4: 11 - 15

11 So Christ himself gave some to be apostles, some to be prophets, some to be evangelists, pastors, and teachers,

12 to equip his people for works of service, so that the body of Christ may be built up

13 until we all reach unity in the faith and in the knowledge of the Son of God and become mature, attaining to the whole measure of the fullness of Christ.

14 Then we will no longer be infants, tossed back and forth by the waves, and blown here and there by every wind of teaching and by the cunning and craftiness of people in their deceitful scheming.

15 Instead, speaking the truth in love, **we will grow to become in every respect the mature body** of him who is the head, that is, Christ.

Verse: 14 speaks of no longer being infants but mature Christians led by the Holy Spirit so we don't fall to the false teaching of deceived people.

It can't be said enough, we need all of these gifts in operation within the church if we ever hope to become the church God intended.

Again I have to ask where are the Apostles and Prophets?

Look at the scriptures in 1 Corinthians 12 and you will see what I mean.

1 Corinthians 12: 27 – 31

27 <u>Now you are the body of Christ, and each one of you is a part of it.</u>

28 And <u>God has placed in the church first of all apostles, second prophets, third teachers, then miracles, then gifts of healing, of helping, of guidance, and of different kinds of tongues.</u>

29 Are all apostles? Are all prophets? Are all teachers? Do all work miracles?

30 Do all have gifts of healing? Do all speak in tongues? Do all interpret?

31 **<u>Now eagerly desire the greater gifts.</u>** And yet I will show you the most excellent way.

Look also at Ephesians 2: 20

20 <u>built on the foundation of the apostles and prophets, with Christ Jesus himself as the chief cornerstone.</u>

Let this sink in. We have Pastors, Teachers, and Evangelist operating within the church but what about the Apostles and Prophets.

According to these scriptures, if we were to build a house with these two essential pieces missing we wouldn't have a very sturdy structure and if the foundation is missing key parts what would be the condition of the rest of the house?

As with most houses, they look great from the outside, at first, then you start looking closer. The corners start to settle and the plaster starts to crack, the windows and doors won't open and close right. Then you notice the floors aren't level and the plumbing starts to leak because of stress on the pipes because the walls are shifting and the cabinets in the kitchen aren't straight because of the walls being out of plumb. All of this will happen because we forgot two major parts of the foundation, and the same has happened within the church.

So what does all this have to do with the Last Days? Remember what Jesus had to say; "Watch out that no one deceives you" and there is a good chance we have been deceived, either knowingly or unknowingly!

Jesus doesn't paint a very pretty picture. Oh we know how it ends and sadly we focus on that, not considering what the journey will be like to get us to the end. That is the question!

This gives us a pretty gloomy picture: many deceived, persecuted, put to death, hated, many will turn away from the faith, will betray each other and the love of most will grow cold.

It's no wonder the church wants to be raptured before the Great Tribulation. No one in their right mind would want to go through these things and this is talking about the church!

We need to understand why these things must happen, remember what John the Baptist said about Jesus. He will baptize you with the Holy Spirit and with fire, along with the Holy Spirit comes great power but what comes with Fire?

Matthew 3:11, Luke 3:16

Daniel 12: 10

Many will be purified, made spotless and refined, but the wicked will continue to be wicked. None of the wicked will understand, **but those who are wise will understand.**

Now, do you understand why these things must happen? For anyone to truly be able to handle the power of the Holy Spirit, we need to be prepared; we need to be Purified!

We think we are so mature and ready. Don't we operate with the power of the Holy Spirit? That might be true to a point, but you haven't seen anything yet!! We have seen glimpses of the awesome power of God but they are nothing in comparison to what is yet to come.

I have experienced some miraculous workings of the Holy Spirit! I have also seen my failures in my misunderstanding of God's ways, yet he used me. It still amazes me how he speaks to us and sometimes just a knowing that can't be explained. If we are to mature we need to be in a place where we can experience and operate in the gifts of the Holy Spirit, without fear or condemnation.

It's a learning process: trial, and error!

Maybe error isn't the right term to be used here. I like the analogy Thomas Edison is supposed to have said about the light bulb. He wasn't going to give up on how to make a light bulb, for he already came up with hundreds of ways how NOT to make a light bulb.

The point is, we learn from our mistakes. We learn what doesn't work and know not to do it that way again, just like Edison and the light bulb.

Remember we are dealing with the Spiritual and the only handbook or manual written on the subject is the Bible and it only gives us the basics of who and how the Holy Spirit can and will operate. From that point on, it's the individual's place to learn and mature in the ways of the Holy Spirit and we are told to go to our Counselor for that advice. We are told to test the spirit. In other words, is that the right spirit or the wrong spirit, the right way or the wrong way!

It's time to knock on the Counselor's door!

Where to next?

Matthew 24: 13,14

13 but the one who stands firm to the end will be saved.

14 And this gospel of the kingdom will be preached in the whole world as a testimony to all nations, and then the end will come.

Here we see some Hope, if we are firm in our Faith to the End we will be saved.

Next is an important part of these times, "This gospel of the Kingdom being preached in the whole world", just one more prophecy to be fulfilled, no the Rapture will not be happening today!

Then and only then will events be right for the end to come!

With our vast knowledge and worldwide communications hasn't that already happened? The Gospel is being transmitted all over the world through radio and the internet. Everyone can hear it, can't they?

Over the past twenty-some years, I have belonged to a group called Christian Boaters Association. Through this group I have friends who are part of Wycliffe Bible Translators who support teams of translators all over the world. Little known families who will spend years learning a particular dialect of a little known language in some remote part of the world to give them a Bible in their own language. The sacrifice of these people so the Gospel can be spread throughout the world. There are literally thousands of different languages and various dialects of these languages. But through the efforts of Wycliffe Bible Translators and other groups, these numbers are dwindling and the fulfillment of Jesus' words is coming close to completion.

Other groups are working toward bringing the Jewish people back to their homeland, Israel. Aliyah is another fulfillment of Bible prophecy. These people work tirelessly behind the scenes and in obscure places to assist God's chosen people to return home.

An interesting note; at the time of this writing, there are now more Jewish people living in Israel, their own homeland, than another country in the world. Up until this time the United States has had the largest number of Jewish people living here, but now this is not true. Over the years, we have had several Jewish friends move to Israel and now have friends living in Jerusalem.

We are now up to verse 15 of Matthew 24, and to put it mildly, things get real serious from this point on.

Oh! We aren't here at this point, Right?

Humor me, lets read on; as you read pay particular attention to verses 22 and 24 where it talks about the Elect. Who are they? Now if

I read the scriptures correctly, we are the Elect, the chosen, whether by birth or by adoption.

Another point concerning verse 15, and we can also read in Daniel and Revelation where it is referenced to as the midpoint in the Great Tribulation. Jesus is putting a particular emphasis on this as He says; "Let the reader understand." And he goes on to what we are to do and not do and the conditions of that time. False messiahs and false prophets are saying, "Go here or go there." This again calls for discernment!

Matthew 24: 15

15 "So when you see standing in the holy place **'the abomination that causes desolation,'** spoken of through the prophet Daniel—**let the reader understand—**

Again we read in the book of Daniel;

Daniel 11: 31 – 35

31 "His armed forces will rise up to desecrate the temple fortress and will abolish the daily sacrifice. Then they will set up the abomination that causes desolation.

32 With flattery, he will corrupt those who have violated the covenant, but the people who know their God will firmly resist him.

33 "Those who are wise will instruct many, though for a time they will fall by the sword or be burned or captured or plundered.

34 When they fall, they will receive a little help, and many who are not sincere will join them.

35 Some of the wise will stumble, so that they may be refined, purified and made spotless until the time of the end, for it will still come at the appointed time.

Matthew 24: 16 - 20

16 then let those who are in Judea flee to the mountains.

17 Let no one on the housetop go down to take anything out of the house.

18 Let no one in the field go back to get their cloak.

19 How dreadful it will be in those days for pregnant women and nursing mothers!

20 Pray that your flight will not take place in winter or on the Sabbath.

Let's examine these verses for a moment. Those in Judea are to flee to the mountains, and are to take nothing with them. Then he says to pray that your flight will not take place in the winter or on the Sabbath. Now everything here is referring to fleeing in a hurry, but to where?

Now let's look at some other scriptures in the book of Revelation.

Revelation 12: 6 - 12

6 <u>**The woman fled into the wilderness to a place prepared for her by God, where she might be taken care of for 1,260 days.**</u>

7 Then war broke out in heaven. Michael and his angels fought against the dragon, and the dragon and his angels fought back.

8 But he was not strong enough, and they lost their place in heaven.

9 The great dragon was hurled down—that ancient serpent called the devil, or Satan, who leads the whole world astray. He was hurled to the earth, and his angels with him.

Remember we do not know what the Seven Thunders had to say as it was sealed up, but here it is referring to the Woman fleeing into the wilderness to a place prepared for her for 3 ½ years.

What do we have left after the abomination that causes desolation is revealed?

3 ½ years, Hum-mm?

Now the real question is - who is the Woman? Could it be the Bride of Christ, the Church? I think for the most part many refer to her as Israel but remember, we are chosen, adopted into God's chosen people, Israel! As I look at, there are so many connections and possibilities here in Revelation 12.

Could it be that when Satan loses the battle in heaven and is hurled down to earth, is the same time as when the abomination which causes desolation is set up in the Temple?

10 Then I heard a loud voice in heaven say: "Now have come the salvation and the power and the kingdom of our God, and the authority of his Messiah. <u>For the accuser of our brothers and sisters,</u> who accuses them before our God day and night, has been hurled down.

11 <u>**They triumphed over him by the blood of the Lamb and by the word of their testimony; they did not love their lives so much as to shrink from death.**</u>

12 Therefore rejoice, you heavens and you who dwell in them!

There are two things here. First, we see Satan kicked out of heaven and hurled to the earth. Then we are talking about our brothers and sisters who have died for their faith.

Matthew 24: 21 - 27

21 For then there will be great distress, unequaled from the beginning of the world until now—and never to be equaled again.

22 <u>**"If those days had not been cut short, no one would survive, but for the sake of the elect those days will be shortened.**</u>

23 At that time if anyone says to you, 'Look, here is the Messiah!' or, 'There he is!' do not believe it.

24 For false messiahs and false prophets will appear and perform great signs and wonders <u>to deceive, if possible, even the elect.</u>

25 <u>See, I have told you ahead of time.</u>

26 "So if anyone tells you, 'There he is, out in the wilderness,' do not go out; or, 'Here he is, in the inner rooms,' do not believe it.

27 For as lightning that comes from the east is visible even in the west, so will be the coming of the Son of Man.

There are several issues of understanding we need to look at here.

First, who is the Bible written to? As a simple answer the Old Testament was written for Israel and the New Testament was written for the Church. Now because of the family connection between Israel and the Church, the Church uses both the Old and New Testaments of the Bible. To put it a little clearer the Bible was written for you and me.

So when it says, "You" it literally means, "You"!

Secondly, the term "Elect", is used two times in these scriptures, first in verse 22 and again in verse 24. over the years I have heard several explanations. "Who is the elect"?

From these scriptures it is apparent the "Elect" hold great favor with God. In verse 22, it says, "But for the sake of the elect those days will be shortened." Because of God's great concern for the well being of the Elect, He is shortening the time of His wrath. Then in verse 24 it tells us of the "great signs and wonders" that will be performed by "FALSE" messiahs and prophets. These signs and wonders are so convicting that most people will be deceived by them, but by the discernment of the Holy Spirit the "Elect" will see the deception.

Now, we know Israel is God's chosen people and we also know through Christ we have been adopted into Israel. But we also know not every Jew will be called by God, only those who accept Jesus. So it has to be clear the "Elect" are the Jews and Gentiles who have accepted Jesus as their "Messiah"

Then Jesus says, "See, I have told **you** ahead of time." Jesus is saying don't be surprised by these things, they are going to happen. Who is He telling? **"YOU!"**

So, we have come the point of looking into those scriptures in the Book of Revelation which gives us some insight into the events of the Last Days.

Revelation 2: 10, 11

10 Do not be afraid of what you are about to suffer. I tell you, the devil will put some of you in prison to test you, and you will suffer persecution for ten days. Be faithful, even to the point of death, and I will give you life as your victor's crown.

11 Whoever has ears, let them hear what the Spirit says to the churches. The one who is victorious will not be hurt at all by the second death.

As we know this letter is written to the church in Smyrna but what we don't know is when this happens. The general consensus is that it has already happened, but being part of the Book of Revelation, does it have a two part meaning? Many believe the letters written to the seven churches are a warning for the church today!

Verse 11, should get your attention, "Whoever has ears, (do we have spiritual ears?), let them hear what the Spirit says to the churches." Only with spiritual ears can we hear and discern what the Holy Spirit is saying.

Revelation 3: 10

10 Since you have kept My command to endure patiently, <u>I will also keep you from the hour of trial</u> that is going to come on the whole world to test the inhabitants of the earth.

Revelation 6: 9 - 11

9 <u>When he opened the fifth seal, I saw under the altar the souls of those who had been slain because of the word of God and the testimony they had maintained.</u>

10 They called out in a loud voice, "How long, Sovereign Lord, holy and true, until you judge the inhabitants of the earth and avenge our blood?"

11 **<u>Then each of them was given a white robe, and they were told to wait a little longer, until the full number of their fellow servants, their brothers, and sisters, were killed just as they had been.</u>**

Revelation 7: 3 - 8

3 **<u>"Do not harm the land or the sea or the trees until we put a seal on the foreheads of the servants of our God."</u>**

4 <u>Then I heard the number of those who were sealed:</u> 144,000 from all the tribes of Israel.

5 From the tribe of Judah 12,000 were sealed, from the tribe of Reuben 12,000, from the tribe of Gad 12,000,

6 from the tribe of Asher 12,000, from the tribe of Naphtali 12,000, from the tribe of Manasseh 12,000,

7 from the tribe of Simeon 12,000, from the tribe of Levi 12,000, from the tribe of Issachar 12,000,

8 from the tribe of Zebulun 12,000, from the tribe of Joseph 12,000, from the tribe of Benjamin 12,000.

The 144,000 has always been of great controversy. It says what it says but I would ask this question; the twelve tribes of Israel, where are they? We know they were scattered all over Europe and who knows where else? I don't have any idea as to the answer, but I will ask another question. What is in your DNA? Are you a descendant of these lost tribes of Israel and since we have been adopted into Israel, which tribe do we belong to? As I see it, there are no real answers to these questions, maybe? Another thought. Are we dealing with actual numbers or are they symbolic or something which will be revealed in the days ahead? The book of Revelation has so much we can't understand until God reveals it to us.

Revelation 7: 9, 13 - 15

9 After this, I looked, and there before me was a great multitude that no one could count, from every nation, tribe, people and language, standing before the throne and before the Lamb. They were wearing white robes and were holding palm branches in their hands.

13 Then one of the elders asked me, **"These in white robes—who are they, and where did they come from?"**

14 I answered, "Sir, you know." And he said, **"These are they who have come out of the Great Tribulation;** they have washed their robes and made them white in the blood of the Lamb.

15 Therefore, "they are before the throne of God and serve him day and night in his temple; and he who sits on the throne will shelter them with his presence.

Here we find a group of people so large that they couldn't be counted and we are told they came out of the Great Tribulation. Who are they? Verse 14 tells us they are Christians who came out of the Great Tribulation!

Revelation 13: 3 – 10

3 One of the heads of the beast seemed to have had a fatal wound, but the fatal wound had been healed. The whole world was filled with wonder and followed the beast.

4 People worshiped the dragon because he had given authority to the beast, and they also worshiped the beast and asked, "Who is like the beast? Who can wage war against it?"

5 <u>The beast was given a mouth to utter proud words and blasphemies and **to exercise its authority for forty-two months.**</u>

6 It opened its mouth to blaspheme God and to slander his name and his dwelling place and those who live in heaven.

7 **<u>It was given power to wage war against God's holy people and to conquer them.</u>** And it was given authority over every tribe, people, language and nation.

8 **<u>All inhabitants of the earth will worship the beast—all whose names have not been written in the Lamb's book of life, the Lamb who was slain from the creation of the world.</u>**

9 **<u>Whoever has ears, let them hear.</u>**

10 **<u>"If anyone is to go into captivity, into captivity they will go. If anyone is to be killed with the sword, with the sword they will be killed."This calls for patient endurance and faithfulness on the part of God's people.</u>**

Here we go, the beast is exercising his authority for forty-two months, (three and one-half years) to wage war against who? God's holy people, those whose names have been written in the Lamb's book of life. (The "Elect")

Then in verse 9 we are given a warning which we heard before, or a, 'are you hearing me'? Then he goes on (verse 10) to tell us God has a plan and purpose for each of us and we need to trust in him, with patient endurance and faithfulness.

Revelations 20: 4 - 6

4 I saw thrones on which were seated those who had been given authority to judge. **And I saw the souls of those who had been beheaded because of their testimony about Jesus and because of the word of God. They had not worshiped the beast or its image and had not received its mark on their foreheads or their hands. They came to life and reigned with Christ a thousand years.**

5 (The rest of the dead did not come to life until the thousand years were ended.)

This is the first resurrection.

6 Blessed and holy are those who share in the first resurrection. The second death has no power over them, but they will be priests of God and of Christ and will reign with him for a thousand years.

As I see it, Revelation 20 sums it up. If you ever had any question concerning when the Rapture or Second Coming was going to take place, here is the answer. In verse 4, it spells it out very clearly, the ones who will go thru the Great Tribulation are a part of the First Resurrection.

How I wish I could say with a clear conscience that we are not going to be here during the Great Tribulation. I don't have all the answers but there are so many dots that connect which points to the First Resurrection being at the end of the Great Tribulation.

With the warnings Jesus is giving us; "Watch out that no one Deceives you", "Let the Reader Understand", "Whoever has ears, let them hear", there is something here we need to pay attention to because it is for our benefit.

If the question still stands as to when the Rapture takes place or the Second Coming as the scriptures call it. Let's look at another scripture in the Book of Acts;

Acts 1: 8 – 11

8 But you will receive power when the Holy Spirit comes on you, and you will be my witnesses in Jerusalem, and in all Judea and Samaria, and to the ends of the earth."

9 After he said this, <u>he was taken up before their very eyes, and a cloud hid him from their sight.</u>

10 They were looking intently up into the sky <u>as he was going</u>, when suddenly two men dressed in white stood beside them.

11 "Men of Galilee," they said, "why do you stand here looking into the sky? <u>This same Jesus, who has been taken from you into heaven, will come back in the same way you have seen him go into heaven."</u>

Here is an important clue concerning the return of Jesus, another dot to connect. Pay particular attention to what the two angels said; Jesus will return in the same way you saw him go into heaven.

Now back up to verse 9, Jesus was standing with them, talking to them and all of a sudden He was taken up from the earth before their very eyes and a cloud hid Him from their sight.

So for Jesus' return, he will appear in the clouds and come down to the earth, just the reverse of the way he went into heaven. Not appear in the clouds with all the dead in Christ to then turn around and go back to heaven, it does not say that!

Another question; why would Jesus bring all the dead in Christ with him only to turn around and take everyone back to heaven? I think it would make better sense if he was returning (Second Coming) to bring the dead in Christ with him and we who are still alive who have just been changed from our physical bodies to our spiritual bodies to go meet him in the sky.

1 Thessalonians 4: 14

For we believe that Jesus died and rose again, and so we believe that God will bring with Jesus those who have fallen asleep in him.

Think about this; when we are expecting company to visit our home, and when we see them coming down the road or in the driveway, don't we go out to meet them? Especially when we have waited so long for them to arrive. The excitement of the wait has been building and we run out the door to go meet them as they arrive. We do it all the time.

Can you imagine the wondrous joy of Jesus' return? We are talking about the event of eternity, a moment when we, as mortals, receive our spiritual bodies, as scripture says "We go to meet Him in the air", In other words, "We Can Fly!" In the excitement of the moment, we can't wait to be with Jesus, to look into the heavens and see Jesus surrounded by a host of such magnitude that they fill the heavens. As the words of the song says, "I Can Only Imagine". To think about what is going to happen stirs my spirit and gives me goosebumps just writing about it!

After looking at these verses and the verses of Revelation 20, it became pretty apparent as to when the First Resurrection takes place, for we see those who were beheaded and didn't receive the mark of the beast during the Great Tribulation. They are a part of the First Resurrection, so the events surrounding 1 Thessalonians 4: 17 has to take place at the end of the seven years.

Now I am sure there are going to be those who will say the Rapture is different than the First Resurrection. How can that be? When the dead in Christ are brought back with Jesus and we are changed from physical bodies to spiritual bodies, that is the First Resurrection! Think about it. Our spiritual bodies can fly! Now that is a Resurrection I want to be a part of!

Throughout these scriptures there are warnings after warnings to be prepared. Get your Bibles out and read these verses. As Jesus said, "Watch out that no one deceives you", and that includes me!

I can not tell you how these events are going to all connect, but I can assure you that until the appointed time, no man is going to know. Sure we can speculate, make long flowing charts and write long elaborate books on the subject but there is no way we can truly give an accurate summary of how it's going to happen. The only thing we can do is look at the individual event and say with some accuracy, "This is going to happen." Then we must trust in God and His Word.

I have put a lot of scriptures before you and for some, these are new ideas and I understand that, but this is the Word of God straight from the Bible.

We can not neglect these scriptures just because they don't fit into our traditions or doctrines, we have to deal with them. I have an obligation to present these scriptures to you and it is your choice and responsibility to read and seek the Guidance Counselor, the Holy Spirit.

"Watch out no one Deceives you"

The "I Am"

Over years of experiences, I am still amazed as to how little we know about God and the more I see and experience, the more I realize how much we take for granted.

When we think of God, we call Him Lord, Father, God Most High, The Almighty, Creator, Mighty Father, Awesome, and so much more, for that is what we have been trained to do or what we find written in the Bible.

What do we picture when we think of God; this majestic gray-haired man sitting on a throne of gold surrounded by multitudes of angels?

But what do we really know or think we know about Him? Let's start with three simple descriptions from the Bible;

God is Creator

Genesis 14:19 - and he blessed Abram, saying, "Blessed be Abram by God Most High, **Creator of heaven and earth.**

Genesis 14:22 - But Abram said to the king of Sodom, "With raised hand I have sworn an oath to the LORD, God Most High, **Creator of heaven and earth,**

Deuteronomy 32:6 - Is this the way you repay the LORD, you foolish and unwise people? Is he not your Father, your **Creator, who made you and formed you?**

To think everything we know and can conceivably comprehend was created by God, "God said let there be light". . . God said it and it was!

To create in its self is enough to overload our minds, how do you create something? We create a pie or cake from scratch, but we take all of the ingredients which already exist and we follow the recipe to make something, that is how we create something.

I had an idea in my mind of a house I wanted to build, I drew up plans, figured the materials and the cost but for some reason I wasn't able to speak that house into existence. I had to go buy the materials and after a few months of sweat I had it under roof. We are not God, we fall under the sins of Adam and we have to work for our being.

Genesis 3: 17 - 19

17 To Adam, he said, "Because you listened to your wife and ate fruit from the tree about which I commanded you, 'You must not eat from it,' "Cursed is the ground because of you; <u>through painful toil,</u> you will eat food from it all the days of your life.

18 It will produce thorns and thistles for you, and you will eat the plants of the field.

19 <u>By the sweat of your brow</u>, you will eat your food until you return to the ground since from it you were taken; for dust you are and to dust, you will return."

But scripture tells us God spoke it into existence, God took nothing as we perceive it in our understanding and here again we need to remember God's ways are not our ways. Scriptures tell us the wisdom of man is but foolishness in God's eyes.

Here is another interesting thought; verse 19, for it says man was formed from the dust of the earth and from previous scriptures we know the animals were too. An interesting point; Eve was formed from one of Adam's rib as a helpmate. It is no wonder men look at the beauty of a woman and desires her for they are looking at a part of themselves. Doesn't it say to love your wife as yourself, look at the connection! Man was formed from the earth and indirectly Woman was also formed from the earth but through Adam and it says the wife's desires will be for her husband, what a connection!

Who can comprehend the plan of God in his creation? Scientist have been trying for centuries and still don't have the answers.

After seven eye surgeries I have pondered the complexities of the eye. How does something so complicated just happen, how does the eye recognize color, shapes, movement? How do these responses transmit to the brain to compute into a thought that our body responds to and the reverse? We feel hot on our hand and it is transmitted to our brain and our eyes see that our hand is in the fire and tells the brain, get the hand out of the fire. Don't even bother to tell me this just evolved from something out of a swamp.

So while we are on the subject of evolution I will ask another question; where are all the fossil evidence of these millions of years of evolution, there aren't any! I think God put some of these fossils in different places just to play with the minds of peoples, I know if I were God I would! I think God has a sense of humor and if you don't believe me just look in the mirror! Sorry, I just had to say that! Smile it won't hurt!

God is Love

John 3: 16 - For God so loved the world that he gave his one and only Son, that whoever believes in him shall not perish but have eternal life.

1 Corinthians 2:9 - However, as it is written: "What no eye has seen, what no ear has heard, and what no human mind has conceived" — the things God has prepared for those who love him—

1 John 4: 8- Whoever does not love does not know God, because **God is love**.

1 John 4:9 - This is how God showed his love among us: He sent his one and only Son into the world that we might live through him.

1 John 4:12- No one has ever seen God; but if we love one another, God lives in us and His love is made complete in us.

1 John 4:16 - And so we know and rely on the love God has for us. **God is love**. Whoever lives in love lives in God, and God in them.

Love is such a unique thing, it can transcend all other emotions, it will change your life, it can not only give you a different perspective on life but will make you look at how you think and feel about others.

Let me use myself as an example; Bonnie and I knew each other almost all our lives, we went through 11 years of school one grade apart, ran around Flintstone with the same group of kids, went to some of the same parties, played spin the bottle, and probably even kissed with no attraction.

Then after going our separate ways, we are again thrown together at a friend's house, in the middle of a snowstorm, when I walked her home. I don't know why I walked her home that night? But something happened! The God of Love intervened! God's Plan!

Galatians 5 gives us a comparison between the fruits of the flesh and the fruits of the Spirit,

Galatians 5: 16 - 26

16 So I say, walk by the Spirit, and you will not gratify the desires of the flesh.

17 For the flesh desires what is contrary to the Spirit, and the Spirit what is contrary to the flesh. They are in conflict with each other so that you are not to do whatever you want.

18 But if you are led by the Spirit, you are not under the law.

19 The Acts of the flesh are obvious: sexual immorality, impurity, and debauchery;

20 idolatry and witchcraft; hatred, discord, jealousy, fits of rage, selfish ambition, dissensions, factions

21 and envy; drunkenness, orgies, and the like. I warn you, as I did before, that those who live like this will not inherit the kingdom of God. But the Fruit of the Spirit is love, joy, peace, forbearance, kindness, goodness, faithfulness,

23 gentleness and self-control. Against such things, there is no law.

24 Those who belong to Christ Jesus have crucified the flesh with its passions and desires.

25 Since we live by the Spirit, let us keep in step with the Spirit.

26 Let us not become conceited, provoking and envying each other.

In verses 19 – 21 we find the Fruits of the Flesh, listing 15 different things and verse 26 adds three more. All of which gratify self in some way, its all about me, sound familiar? Just watch the commercials on TV today, its all about me, I deserve it, it's my time and the universe revolves around me. Just ask me!

This is what is going on in our country today, a false doctrine is being taught in a very subtle way telling everyone they deserve more without working for it.

Then we go to the Fruits of the Spirit, listed in verses 22 & 23, as you read each of them you will find they don't deal with self but how we interact with others.

I find it interesting that the first one listed is Love and if you think about it, all of the others hinge on the very first one, as scriptures say, "Love conquers All". These fruits can only come from a God of Love.

No matter how you play it the Flesh will lead you to sin and death. But the Fruits of the Spirit will set you free from the bondage's of the flesh. Only a loving God can make those changes for we were born into sin, its in our DNA you can't escape it any other way.

Only through the blood of Jesus and what He did on the cross!

God is Spirit

John 4: 24 – God is Spirit and his worshipers must worship in the Spirit and in truth."

Now John is the only one to give us the definitive statement, "God is Spirit" and I am not so quick to run with a single statement from scripture when we don't have confirmation of others.

So how do we look at this scripture, do we take it on its own merit or are there other scriptures which back it up? Can we confirm in fact that God is Spirit?

First, let's look at the Trinity, Three in One; God the Father, God the Son, Jesus, and God the Holy Spirit. All the same, but different.

Remember God sent His Son Jesus as a man, in the flesh but what was He before He was sent to the earth for our salvation, Spirit?

The Holy Spirit is an interesting place to start, by His very name we assume we know that He is spirit because it is part of His name. When it comes down to it you can't talk about one part of the Trinity without talking about them all.

What else does the Bible tell us about the Spirit of God which could help us understand who or what he is?

Genesis 1: 1, 2

1 In the beginning, God created the heavens and the earth.

2 Now the earth was formless and empty, darkness was over the surface of the deep, <u>and the Spirit of God was hovering over the waters.</u>

From the very start, the Holy Spirit was present, it says the Spirit of God was hovering over the water, could this be another confirmation when it says "the Spirit of God" a part of God, a part of the Trinity?

What do you expect when you are at the sea shore or on the water? You experience wind or a breeze off the ocean.

Air is accentual for life as we know it. Some translations use the word "Wind" in place of "Spirit of God" and yet other translations use the word "Moved over the water" in place of "Hovered or Hovering over the water".

We have such a unique situation here on earth, the air is held on the surface of the earth by a thin layer called Ozone, to be used and regenerated by people and plants, Amazing! To think some people believe this happened by lucky circumstances, a self-sustaining environment where plants and animals co-exist dependent on each other just happened in the precise combination of elements without a master plan, what are the odds?

Genesis 1: 26 & 27

26 Then God said, "<u>Let us make mankind in our image, in our likeness,</u> so that they may rule over the fish in the sea and the birds in the sky, over the livestock and all the wild animals, and over all the creatures that move along the ground."

27 <u>So God created mankind in his own image, in the image of God he created them;</u> male and female he created them.

So from these verses, we can say God looks like us for he made us in his own image, he created us.

Genesis 3:

Then the LORD God formed a man from the dust of the ground and <u>breathed into his nostrils the breath of life</u>, and the man became a living being.

John 20: 19 -23

19 On the evening of that first day of the week, when the disciples were together, with the doors locked for fear of the Jewish leaders, Jesus came and stood among them and said, "Peace be with you!"

20 After he said this, he showed them his hands and side. The disciples were overjoyed when they saw the Lord.

21 Again Jesus said, "Peace be with you! <u>As the Father has sent me, I am sending you.</u>"

22 <u>And with that, he breathed on them and said, "Receive the Holy Spirit.</u>

23 If you forgive anyone's sins, their sins are forgiven; if you do not forgive them, they are not forgiven."

As we read the doors were locked so no one could get in and Jesus all of a sudden is standing among them, here is Jesus in his Glorified Body (A Spiritual Body) and can move freely about where ever he pleased, yet appears to them in the flesh. After His greeting and commissioning of His disciples, it says, "<u>He breathed on them</u>", saying, "<u>Receive the Holy Spirit</u>". What was it He breathed on them or would it be possible to say He blew air on them?

Air is what we breathe. Now think of this; until now the Disciples did not have the Holy Spirit and at this moment the Holy Spirit was given to them, transferred to them in the air Jesus breathed on them. Jesus' words conveyed the Holy Spirit, "Jesus said it, so that settles it", at that moment the Disciples breathed in and the Holy Spirit was transferred to them. In the Air we Breath!

Now, this is only an idea of mine but we see an association between the wind, air, breath and the Holy Spirit. How simplified it would be for the Holy Spirit to be in the air we breath or is the Wind!

According to scripture he residences in us and what better way than in the air. Think about the part air (Oxygen) plays in our body, we breath it in filling our lungs where it purifies our blood, what a connection!

Acts 2:1 - 8

1 In my former book, Theophilus, I wrote about all that Jesus began to do and to teach

2 until the day he was taken up to heaven, <u>after giving instructions through the Holy Spirit to the apostles he had chosen.</u>

3 After his suffering, he presented himself to them and gave many convincing proofs that he was alive. He appeared to them over a period of forty days and spoke about the kingdom of God.

4 On one occasion, while he was eating with them, he gave them this command: "Do not leave Jerusalem but wait for the gift my Father promised, which you have heard me speak about.

5 For John baptized with water, but in a few days you will be baptized with the Holy Spirit."

6 Then they gathered around him and asked him, "Lord, are you at this time going to restore the kingdom to Israel?"

7 He said to them: "It is not for you to know the times or dates the Father has set by his own authority.

8 But you will receive power when the Holy Spirit comes on you, and you will be my witnesses in Jerusalem, and in all Judea and Samaria, and to the ends of the earth."

I believe here is a point which is missed by many, for the Disciples had already received the Holy Spirit when Jesus breathed on them and now He is telling them to wait for the Baptism of the Holy Spirit, two entirely different experiences. It will be hard for some to accept this for they have been taught the Holy Spirit was not given until Pentecost but when Jesus said, "Receive the Holy Spirit" it happened, think about it, contrary to what we have been taught, when Jesus spoke it, it had to happen!

In the initial act of Salvation, we confess our sins and our acceptance of Jesus, we believe in him and at that moment the Holy Spirit comes and lives within us, we receive the Holy Spirit.

As Jesus is telling his Disciples to wait for yet another experience, the Baptism of the Holy Spirit. At which time they will receive Power when the Holy Spirit comes on them and they will be his witnesses to the ends of the earth.

I can not say it enough, we are missing so much by our negligence of the things of the Holy Spirit, we have Socialized him out of the Church. What do I mean by Socialized, well lets put it this way, we mean well by our programs and out reach projects, our food banks and clothing giveaway's, these are things we need to be doing and do. But when it takes the place of maturing the Saints, of reaching Unity and most importantly Spiritual Growth and Maturity. If we don't train in the church, then where?

The Church needs to be a place where the Saints can come and learn by experience how to discern and test the things of the Spirit, where they can make mistakes and learn from those mistakes. I have always said we learn more from our mistakes then we do from our accomplishments. It is imperative we learn to "Walk in the Spirit" as the days get closer to the Second Coming of Christ.

As we know this is a walk of Faith in God and there are many things we will never know in this life time, but we need to be in an environment where we can experience the Holy Spirit.

Some years ago we attended a church which was part of a larger organization. They held their annual leadership conference in Cincinnati, Ohio. Here was the most amazing Prophetic Workshops I have ever been a part of and experienced. Led by a group of proven Prophets, anyone could go to be prayed for, Yes, prophesied over by a number of Prophets.

Broken into groups of three or four Prophets, each group recorded every thing said, giving a copy to the individual and a master tape was kept for future reference. I wrote about this before but what a blessing for the body of Christ, I can't tell you how it touched me.

Again this is just one of the gifts of the Holy Spirit but Paul put certain emphasis on Prophecy in his letters to the church of Corinth.

1 Corinthians 14: 1

Follow the way of love and eagerly desire gifts of the Spirit, <u>especially prophecy.</u>

1 Corinthians 14: 39, 40

Therefore, my brothers and sisters, <u>be eager to prophesy</u>, and do not forbid speaking in tongues.

40 <u>But everything should be done in a fitting and orderly way.</u>

Remember the Church in Corinth was just learning how to, "Walk in the Spirit" and the Gifts of the Spirit. Especially in chapter 14 much instruction was given to them on the Gift of Prophecy. They were making mistakes and Paul was giving them instruction on the proper use. We could expect no less!

If there is no instruction how are we to learn? If there is no instruction and examples to follow how do we know what is expected? I have seen the Gifts of the Spirit stifled in the Church because leadership themselves did not know how to deal with the Gifts of the Spirit. They need to be taught too!

This is one of the main reasons God put in place Elders, having different gifts to oversee the proper operation of the Gifts of the Spirit. A Pastor can't be expected to fill the shoes of all Five Ministries listed in Ephesians 4: 11

Revelation 19: 10

For it is the Spirit of Prophecy who bears testimony to Jesus."

Conclusion

We have explored several aspects of God; God the Creator, the God of Love and God is Spirit.

Over the years it always amazes me of how God seems to show up in the most opportune of times. When we think things are hopeless or the most unexpected of moments. Then there are the times when we are so wrapped up in our own problems and cares, God will reveal himself in the most unusual of ways. In the whisper of a breeze, the horizon surrounding us or that undeniable voice in the middle of the night.

Our ultimate goal should be to seek the guidance of the Holy Spirit. The Bible gives us a guideline of how we should live and Jesus set the examples for us to follow. As scriptures tell us, "Love never fails", "God never fails"

As believer's God has revealed himself to us in some way and the rest is up to us, we have the Bible, we have the Holy Spirit and Jesus gave us examples to follow.

Define spirit; Something we don't see, we can't touch it, we can't smell it, so what is it?

We can't see God but yet He is everywhere, and our understanding is limited. We were able to see Jesus when God sent him to earth as a man, so we would have an example of who God is and how he wants us to live. Jesus said, "If you see me you have seen the Father."

Most everyone has heard the story of Colton Burpo, "Heaven is for Real." The 4-year-old boy who spent time with Jesus and in heaven where he saw people and knew things with no other way to have known.

Sometime after his experience, he saw the painting 8-year-old Akiane Kramarik did of Jesus and confirmed that was a picture of Jesus whom he saw in heaven. Also confirmed by numerous others who said that painting was the Jesus they saw.

Out of the mouths of children, God has revealed himself to humanity. To give an eight-year-old the ability to paint a masterpiece, as she labeled it, "To Paint the Impossible". An unbelievable story of her journey from poverty to a world wide acclaimed Artist. As scriptures tell us, He confound the wise and learned, now revealing through little children.

I believe we now have a picture or likeness of God, Jesus said if you have seen me you have seen the Father. What an awesome story, I believe we are going to see more Revelations in the days ahead and yes, probably out of the mouths of children!

Another example of God using children is in the book, "The Happiest People on Earth." In the early nineteen hundreds a young boy in Armenia was given a vision, he could not read or write, but put on paper what he saw. From this vision the Armenians were told to leave and move to the United States and part of the vision was sealed up for a later date, so much we don't know yet.

One final thought concerning "God is Spirit". Follow the last days of Jesus here on earth, starting with the crucifixion. Jesus' human body is put in a tomb, then on the third day, he is resurrected in his Glorified body or his Spiritual body. Throughout the forty days he would appear anywhere he wanted as we would think the Holy Spirit can do. But Jesus appears in human form that his Disciples could touch yet being able to change from the Spiritual body to human body as he pleased and still being a Spiritual Being. "God is Spirit"!

The Remnant

This word has always intrigued me. Being around my wife and daughter, whom both sew. I am aware of what a Remnant is; the end of a bolt of material usually put on the discount table and sold for a lesser price. Usually too small for any great use and not wanted by most people who are looking for fabric to do a project. As man looks at the Remnant it is of no great value or use, to be discarded!

As we read scripture we find God has a special place for the Remnant, the unusable in God's eyes is what he uses to confound the wise or the world. Why is it that God looks upon the Remnant in some sense with special favor? Look at the scriptural references;

Matthew 7:13

13 "Enter through the narrow gate. For wide is the gate and broad is the road that leads to destruction, and many enter through it.

Romans 9: 27 - Isaiah cries out concerning Israel: "Though the number of the Israelite's be like the sand by the sea, <u>only the remnant will be saved.</u>

Romans 11: 5 - So too, at the present time there is <u>a remnant chosen by grace.</u>

Romans 9

3 For I could wish that I myself were cursed and cut off from Christ for the sake of my people, those of my own race,

4 the people of Israel. Theirs is the adoption to son-ship; theirs the divine glory, the covenants, the receiving of the law, the temple worship and the promises.

5 Theirs are the patriarchs, and from them is traced the human ancestry of the Messiah, who is God over all, forever praised! Amen.

6 It is not as though God's word had failed. **For not all who are descended from Israel are Israel.**

7 Nor because they are his descendants are they all Abraham's children. On the contrary, "It is through Isaac that your offspring will be reckoned."

8 In other words, it is not the children by physical descent who are God's children, but it is the children of the promise who are regarded as Abraham's offspring.

13 Just as it is written: "Jacob I loved, but Esau I hated."

14 What then shall we say? Is God unjust? Not at all!

15 For he says to Moses, "I will have mercy on whom I have mercy, and I will have compassion on whom I have compassion."

16 It does not, therefore, depend on human desire or effort, but on God's mercy.

18 Therefore God has mercy on whom he wants to have mercy, and he hardens whom he wants to harden.

22 What if God, although choosing to show his wrath and make his power known, bore with great patience the objects of his wrath—prepared for destruction?

23 What if he did this to make the riches of his glory known to the objects of his mercy, whom he prepared in advance for glory—

24 even us, whom he also called, not only from the Jews but also from the Gentiles?

25 As he says in Hosea: "I will call them 'my people' who are not my people, and I will call her 'my loved one' who is not my loved one,"

26 and, **"In the very place where it was said to them, 'You are not my people,' there they will be called 'children of the living God.'"**

27 Isaiah cries out concerning Israel: "**Though the number of the Israelite's be like the sand by the sea, only the remnant will be saved.**

The word Remnant is found 64 times within our Bibles and most always in reference to those which the Lord will or have saved. As we have read God's chosen people are not exempt from God's judgments. "Only the Remnant will be Saved!"

FAITHFULNESS of the REMNANT

The Glory of God

Throughout our lives, we might have moments where we experience the presence of the Holy Spirit or an encounter with Jesus!

I can only imagine what it will be like to walk in God's presence.

The sheer magnitude of his radiating Glory, think about it. Moses radiated God's Glory after being in His presence. Even the radiating glory scared the people for Moses had to wear a veil when among them for they couldn't look at his face.

The amazing thing is our hopes of ever being in the presence of God can never be without Jesus shedding his blood, sacrificing himself on our behalf!

Only by the blood of Jesus!

This is what the world does not understand or comprehend. How the fulfillment of God's law by the sacrifice of a perfect lamb can compensate for our sins. Atonement does not fit into a worldly way of thinking. Only by the blood of Jesus, of what he did on the cross! Once for all!

Think about this, anything and everything in the presence of God would have to radiate his Glory, we have only seen glimpses of that Glory in scripture and the personal accounts of the different people.

We read of this glorious place called heaven, the streets glimmering with gold and precious stones of all kinds in the foundation of the buildings. All of which are radiating the Glory of God. In the presence of God, a lump of coal would have to radiate the beauty and Glory of God.

Scripture tells us darkness has no place in God's presence, think about it, there can be no shadows anywhere in God's presence.

Exodus 34

29 When Moses came down from Mount Sinai with the two tablets of the covenant law in his hands, he was not aware that his face was radiant because he had spoken with the LORD.

30 When Aaron and all the Israelite's saw Moses, his face was radiant, and they were afraid to come near him.

If you read the whole chapter you find that Moses kept a veil over his face when he wasn't in the presence of God. It says that he didn't realize he was radiating the Glory of God until he saw the reaction of the people as they were afraid to go near him.

Another example; The shepherds tending their sheep on the night Jesus was born and the angel appeared to them.

Luke 2: 8, 9

And there were shepherds living out in the fields nearby, keeping watch over their flocks at night. <u>An angel of the Lord appeared to them, and the Glory of the Lord shone around them, and they were terrified.</u>

The angel of the Lord radiated the Glory from being in God's presence and it says they were terrified.
Sinful flesh reacting to the Glory of God. Sin can not be in the presence of God, only when covered by the blood of Jesus. Here on a hillside, the shepherds were reacting to just the radiating Glory of the angel who had been in God's presence. Amazing!

The Transfiguration

Matthew 17: 1- 6

1 After six days Jesus took with him Peter, James, and John the brother of James, and led them up a high mountain by themselves.

2 There he was transfigured before them. His face shone like the sun, and his clothes became as white as the light.

3 Just then there appeared before them Moses and Elijah, talking with Jesus.

4 Peter said to Jesus, "Lord, it is good for us to be here. If you wish, I will put up three shelters—one for you, one for Moses and one for Elijah."

5 While he was still speaking, a bright cloud covered them, and a voice from the cloud said, "This is my Son, whom I love; with him, I am well pleased. Listen to him!"

6 When the disciples heard this, they fell facedown to the ground, terrified.

Even from within a cloud the radiating Glory of God terrified them as they couldn't even look up but hid their faces in the ground.

Luke 9: 28 - 32

Luke's writings are slightly different than Matthews as he goes into a little more detail of what happened but the account of encountering the Glory of God is the same..

It never ceases to amaze me how God can open our eyes to something that was always there and we never saw it until now.

But then again we are talking about the things of God and one of the responsibilities of the Holy Spirit is to remind us of Jesus' teachings and to show us things to come.

Notes

As I am writing a thought may come to mine which seems to be beneficial to writing, or for life in general.

As you have noticed there are points I have repeated numerous times which is not without purpose, these are things I believe to be vital for the growth of the Church. I can't stress enough the Word of God and not taking it out of context or conflicting with other scriptures, along with the leading of the Holy Spirit. This is a learning process and if I have missed something please forgive me for I too am human with my faults and failures.

Memories are something we all have but I have found when you try to put them on paper it turns into a task. Something you always knew, now you're not so sure of the exact details and you have to tax your mine to make sure your facts are correct. Details of dates are the hardest; as time goes by somethings that have always been in your memory now are a little foggy and you have to resort to other sources of information to confirm facts or forgotten events.

One of the biggest helps has been the internet and being able to check yearly calendars where I can find what day a date is tied to. Say you wanted to know what day of the week July 4, 1776, was on you can find it. (by the way, it was a Thursday) It makes it a little more personal.

On Thursday, the 4th day of July, 1776, the Continental Congress met in Philadelphia to sign the Declaration of Independence.

Another example is the airplane crash my brother and I was in. It happened on a Thursday but I couldn't remember if it was March 27th or 28th, 2003, I was able to confirm the exact date, March 27th through the internet, a tool with seemingly endless uses.

Why should we write, for my younger years a job resume was

something I had to keep up to date, details of places I worked, when I worked, how long I was employed and my job description.

For the first seven years we were married I changed jobs eight times and in the 26 years I worked as a Ranger I worked at 4 different Parks so it was very important to keep an up to date resume.

My wife's parents wondered if I would ever settle down.

When you get a little older and you have settled into a job these details get all muddled together and it is important to keep a copy of a resume for future reference.

Keeping a journal or diary of major events or places, people you have encountered or visited. Vacations, family happening, surgeries or accidents. All of these things will come in handy at some point in time during your life or a valuable history for your children. How many times have you had to fill out a medical history for a doctor or one of your children needed information about a grandparent of what they died. Or just "maybe!", you might want to write an Autobiography some day.

I have boxes of notes, outlines for sermons and teachings from the time when God spoke to me that I have written, maybe some day I might even put them in order? Or not!

Finding the Peace of God

As I look at the whole thing of writing I realize that each of us has a story. Scripture assures us we have a purpose and with that comes a story.

From my story there are things that happened, things that are not explainable by worldly standards. In the past, I had shared some of these events. Some people have ignored me, changed the subject and even tried to tell me that couldn't happen. I never understood how someone can tell me these things never happened. But as I look closer at their reasoning I realized I had been in the same place. As long as a person can rationalize in their own mind they are right, nothing will change them.

I can remember when my Uncle witnessed to me. I couldn't wait for him to go away!

See, it comes to this point! If we acknowledge there is the slimmest possibility that some truth lies within, then we have to deal with our reasoning why we don't want to accept that thinking. It comes to a perspective of how we deal with truth or do we continue to walk in a lie?

Everyone comes to that point in their lives, Everyone! A moment of decision! God gives us that choice! Free Will, to accept or reject God's plan for our lives.

Everyone has an encounter! The first time I had an encounter with God I didn't know what to do with it, and after time I let it slip away! But for some reason God was merciful and gave me a second chance, this time when He spoke to me there was no second guessing, I Knew!

God's plan was set in place, people, events, timing and purpose.

"Change your life here and now, or you
never get another chance!"

I can't tell you how these words penetrate everything within you! In that instant my life would never be the same again. At that moment I knew the Bible was true, repentance and forgiveness took on a whole new meaning. It can't be put into words what happens in a micro-second with God. Volumes were downloaded into my brain and my spirit, how and why? Only God!

Looking back on some of my life's events, I can see clearly now where God was directing my path. Things I never saw before or fully understood. When and where he put me in the right place, the right people and the right time to accomplish his purpose.

I am ever so humbled to think He did that for me. But see! it wasn't for me, it was to bring Glory to Himself. Explain that one to the world!

With God we come to a point where our lives take on a whole new meaning. We don't have to wonder what our purpose is, who am I or why am I here? It doesn't matter! There is Peace in the journey!

Some people search a life time looking for answers. Travel world over searching for an inter peace that can only come from God through Jesus!

I will never understand the ways of God. How he can orchestrate events to bring me to an out of the way Park to get my attention. The different paths I could have taken. I had a good job as Branch Manager of an Electronics Company. I could have gone to Australia to work on a Radar Tracking Station which had been an interest of mine. To think I was even taking a pay cut to be a Ranger, and as I said before I had turned the job down and God changed my direction and I didn't even realize it, but the peace was there!

Now take a step back and look at the bigger picture, how many people are there in the world? Everyone of these people are interconnected to you and me in some way, we live in a microcosm planned and orchestrated by God, anything and everything works in unison with God's plan.

Genesis 1:1

"In the beginnings God created the heavens and the earth. Now the earth was formless and empty, darkness was over the surface of the deep, and the Spirit of God was hovering over the water."

"And God said!,"

God has a Plan! And that plan can only work for us if we accept His leading and his ways. Oh, we can find other things to try and fill the void, but there will never be a true inter peace without God. That Peace has guided me throughout my life, even when I didn't know it or recognized it.

How do you write a conclusion, when you know there is more to come. Things I don't understand or see at this time. Only by the Spirit of God do I have an inter knowing, which gives me the Peace to take me forward. Only by the Grace of God!

There is so much more I could write but to what end? For the best is yet to come. From God's word, past revelations and as I see God revealing things, I have to wonder, will I ever get to write an ending?

Presumptuous, or, is it God?

The End
"I don't think so!"

Printed in the United States
By Bookmasters